## OF
## BANKRUPTCY TERMS
## FOR COMMERCIAL LENDERS

By

**Brett Anders**
**Jim Bird**
**David Ferguson**
**Dan Flanigan**

**Illustrations by Charlie Podrebarac**

Polsinelli

Shalton | Flanigan | Suelthaus ᴘᴄ

## The Peppercorn Press

Polsinelli makes available the information in this publication (the "Materials") for general informational purposes only. The Materials are not intended to constitute, and do not constitute, legal advice. Moreover, the Materials are not intended to constitute, and do not constitute, a solicitation for the formation of an attorney-client relationship; no attorney-client relationship is created through your use or your receipt of the Materials. Anyone accessing the Materials should not act upon them without first seeking legal counsel. Further, the Materials are general in nature, and may not apply to particular factual or legal circumstances.

## About The Authors

The authors of *The Devil's Dictionary* are members of the Loan Enforcement and Bankruptcy Practice Groups of the Polsinelli law firm, a firm of 300 attorneys (as of March 2007) working from offices in Chicago, Kansas City, New York, St. Louis, Washington, D.C., and other locations. The authors represent their lender clients in bankruptcy courts all over the United States and in a multitude of state and federal courts in foreclosure, receivership, and other extraordinary remedy proceedings. As members of an integrated Financial Services Department whose members routinely represent lenders in sophisticated asset based and other commercial loans and have documented and closed more than 1500 commercial mortgage loans, $11 billion in principal amount, in all 50 states and the District of Columbia, the authors also render extensive advice to their transactional colleagues on enforcement and documentation issues at the loan origination stage.

The *Dictionary* reflects the collective wisdom the authors have gained from their combined total of more than 90 years working in the forefront of real estate and other commercial finance, loan enforcement, financial restructuring, and bankruptcy law. Their collective experience begins even before the adoption of the Bankruptcy Code in 1978, extends through the various upheavals of the 1980's and 1990's (especially the watershed collapse of commercial real estate markets in the late 80's and early 90's), and continues through the securitization era of the late 90's and first decade of this century. They learned their trade in the real estate depression of the late 1980's and early 1990's when they represented major financial institutions struggling to deal with the consequences of the market's collapse. During the mid-1990's they served as primary enforcement counsel for a distressed asset fund consisting of 459 non-performing assets with a book value in excess of $1 billion; in that capacity they handled every conceivable litigation, bankruptcy, and related transactional situation, including forbearance agreements, discounted payoff agreements, loan sales, loan auctions, and operation and disposition of REO. And they have continued to serve both senior and mezzanine lenders during the great expansion of the last decade, litigating from Wall Street to Main Street in traditional defaulted loan cases as well as prepayment, loan fraud, intercreditor, and other litigation.

**Brett Anders** enforces the rights and remedies of secured lenders in state, federal, and bankruptcy courts across the nation. One of his specialties is the use of receivership proceedings to manage, operate, and ultimately sell collateral as an alternative to traditional foreclosure and bankruptcy sales. He also represents CMBS and institutional lenders in lender liability, prepayment, and intercreditor cases. He is listed in *Best Lawyers in America*. Brett can be reached at 816-360-4267 or banders@polsinelli.com.

**Jim Bird** is the chair of Polsinelli's Bankruptcy and Financial Restructuring Practice Group. His practice is focused in the areas of bankruptcy, business reorganizations, business loan workouts, debtor/creditor rights, and insurance company insolvencies. His 25 years of experience in complex bankruptcy and restructuring matters allows him to provide guidance, strategies, and effective solutions to debtor corporations, secured lenders, unsecured creditor committees, debenture holders, shareholders, trustees, and business acquirers. He has acted on behalf of major constituencies in the following notable Chapter 11 cases: Farmland Industries, Inc.; Payless Cashways, Inc. (I and II); Kroh Brothers Development Company; American Freight System, Inc.; Nationsway Transport Service, Inc.; Preston Trucking

Company, Inc.; TransWorld Airlines, Inc.; Global International Airways, Inc.; First Humanics Corporation; Food Barn Stores, Inc.; and CenCor, Inc. He is listed in *Best Lawyers in America*. Jim can be reached 816-360-4343 or jbird@polsinelli.com

**David Ferguson** has practiced law for more than 16 years, focusing his practice on Chapter 11 bankruptcy, creditors' rights, and commercial litigation. He represents a broad array of constituencies in Chapter 11 cases, including lenders, debtors, creditors' committees, landlords, and business acquirers. In addition to his Chapter 11 work, David advocates the rights of lenders in guaranty, loan fraud, lender liability, and other litigation. He can be reached 816-360-4311 or dferguson@polsinelli.com.

**Dan Flanigan** is the Chair of the Polsinelli law firm's Financial Services and Real Estate Department. His practice encompasses all aspects of commercial finance including loan documentation, servicing, and enforcement. He has represented lenders in more than 30 bankruptcy courts throughout the country. Much of his practice currently focuses on the CMBS arena. He served as lead counsel in the formation of two national conduit lenders and advises loan originators and master and special servicers on all aspects of loan structuring, servicing, and enforcement. He is listed in *The Best Lawyers in America*, *Super Lawyers* (Missouri), and *Chambers USA: America's Leading Lawyers*. Dan can be reached 816-360-4260 or dflanigan@polsinelli.com.

## 105 Injunction

The last (and often the first) refuge of a scoundrel (usually, but not always, the debtor).

A bankruptcy court order issued under the allegedly broad powers conferred on the bankruptcy court by Section 105 authorizing the issuance of "any order, process, or judgment that is necessary or appropriate to carry out the provisions of" the Code. Section 105 is cited by debtors and other proponents of a proposed action to justify anything and everything including, for example, critical vendor orders and the grant of injunctions against actions by a lender against guarantors or other co-obligors including permanent injunctions imposed by a debtor's Chapter 11 plan.

*Synonym: Magic Dust.*

Bankruptcy Code § 105.

## 341 Meeting

A meeting convened by the United States Trustee early in a bankruptcy case at which creditors and other parties in interest may question the debtor under oath. Sometimes referred to as "the first meeting of creditors."

If a creditor attempts to actually accomplish something at a 341 meeting, a stern rebuke from the United States Trustee may follow. A creditor's best choice for extracting detailed information under oath from the debtor's representatives is usually a 2004 examination. But a surprise attack at a 341 meeting can be remarkably effective if the U.S Trustee will allow some leeway.

Bankruptcy Code § 341.

## 363 Auction

What the stalking horse (see Stalking Horse) hopes a 363 sale will *not* become. What essentially every other constituency in the case (except perhaps the debtor's management who may have negotiated sweetheart employment agreements with the stalking horse) *will* become.

Although not mandated by the Code or Bankruptcy Rules, it has become standard in Chapter 11 to subject every sale agreement to higher and better offers to be solicited from other potential buyers, culminating in an auction held in open court or in the offices of debtor's counsel.

Bankruptcy Code § 363. See also 363 Sale, Bid Protections, Break-Up Fee, Sale Free and Clear, Stalking Horse, *Sub Rosa* Plan, Topping Fee.

## 363 Sale

The secured creditor's plan of reorganization.

A sale of some or all of the debtor's assets in bankruptcy, a chief feature of which is the debtor's ability to sell assets free and clear of liens and other interests if the debtor can satisfy the relatively liberal requirements of Section 363(f). Often far preferable to the secured creditor than a piecemeal liquidation of the debtor outside of bankruptcy.

Bankruptcy Code § 363. See also 363 Auction, Bid Protections, Break-Up Fee, Sale Free and Clear, Stalking Horse, *Sub Rosa* Plan, Topping Fee.

# 1111(b) Election

The right of a secured creditor that believes its collateral has been under-valued in the bankruptcy process to elect to be treated in a Chapter 11 plan as "fully secured" (in the limited sense discussed in more detail below) rather than partially secured and partially unsecured (see Oversecured Creditor and Undersecured Creditor).

Once upon a time there was a debtor ("Devil's Spawn") who "crammed down" its nonrecourse lender by persuading the bankruptcy court to value the creditor's collateral at millions of dollars less than the loan amount, paying nothing on the unsecured portion of the creditor's claim in Devil's Spawn's Chapter 11 plan (since the claim was, after all, nonrecourse), then selling the property shortly after the confirmation of the plan for more than the creditor's re-valued secured claim and pocketing the difference. The authors of the Bankruptcy Code of 1978 remedied this injustice in two ways—first, by making a nonrecourse claim recourse in Chapter 11 under certain circumstances and, second, by providing secured creditors the 1111(b) election.

The 1111(b) election affords real but limited protection against under-valuation. If the creditor makes the election, the plan must provide for payments to the creditor equal to at least the total amount of its claim. But those payments need only have a present value of at least the court-determined value of the creditor's collateral. Thus, although the electing creditor's claim is initially fully secured by the collateral, it is not entitled to interest on the entire amount of its claim—only on the portion of its claim that would be its secured claim absent the election.

Assume, for example, that a secured creditor is owed a total of $10 million but the court values the creditor's collateral at only $8 million. If the creditor does not make the 1111(b) election and the property is sold the day after the plan becomes effective, the creditor is entitled to receive only $8 million—payment of the court-determined value the collateral. The creditor will receive payment on its $2 million unsecured claim only to the extent provided in the plan. But if the creditor had made the 1111(b) election, it would be entitled to payment of the entire amount of its $10 million claim.

Now assume, however, that the creditor made the 1111(b) election but the property is not sold until one year after the effective date of the plan. Assume further that the creditor is paid under the plan monthly interest only payments at the rate of 10% per annum. The creditor will receive $800,000 in interest payments over the one-year period. The interest payments are, in effect, credited against what might be called the "excess principal" amount of the claim (i.e., the $2 million above the court's $8 million valuation of the creditor's collateral). At the end of the one-year period, the "payoff" amount to the creditor in a sale (including a foreclosure sale) if the creditor made the 1111(b) election would be $9,200,000 ($10 million in principal minus $800,000 in payments). Absent the election, the payoff would be only $8 million, so the creditor would be better off for having made the election (unless the creditor received a return on its unsecured claim under the plan of $1.2 million, a 60% return over a one-year period—not likely!).

Continuing with the example, after 30 months of payments at 10% interest, the creditor would receive interest payments of $2 million and there would no longer be any "excess principal." After that point the creditor would be entitled only to $8 million plus interest. Also at that point, if the creditor had received anything on its unsecured claim, it would have been better off not to have made the election.

Absent the 1111(b) election, an undersecured creditor holds both a secured claim and an unsecured claim in the case, a situation that may enable the undersecured creditor to control voting in the unsecured class of creditors and block confirmation of a plan. This is a strategy designed to defeat confirmation of the plan entirely (the strategy adopted by the great majority of secured creditors in Chapter 11 cases), while the 1111(b) election strategy assumes that a plan that undervalues the creditor's collateral will be confirmed and protects the creditor against that downside. Yet the very existence of 1111(b) operates as a powerful deterrent to the strategy employed by Devil's Spawn.

The 1111(b) election is not available to a secured creditor whose interest in the collateral is of inconsequential value. The election is also not available to a secured creditor whose claim is fully recourse against the debtor and whose collateral is to be sold under a plan or pursuant to Section 363. The creditor must make its 1111(b) election before the conclusion of the hearing on the debtor's disclosure statement (see Disclosure Statement) or within any later time set by the court.

Bankruptcy Code § 1111(b). See also Absolute Priority Rule, Cramdown, Oversecured Creditor, Secured Claim, Undersecured Creditor, Unsecured Claim, Valuation of Collateral.

6

## 2004 Examination

An examination of a witness taken under oath under Bankruptcy Rule 2004. Lender representatives are sometimes subjected to the indignities of this process as creditors search for weaknesses in the creditor's collateral perfection or for causes of action against the lender.

*Synonym: Fishing Expedition.*

## A-B Note Structure

A form of subordinate financing widely used in the CMBS lending arena where a subordinate or "B" Note is secured by the same mortgage as the senior or "A" Note but is deeply subordinated to the "A" Note under an Intercreditor Agreement.

*Diabolical Questions: Has the Darwinian world of real estate finance evolved an even lower order of creature than the unsecured creditor? Will the onerous Intercreditor Agreements they must agree to render the "B" Note holders and other subordinate creditors (see Mezzanine Debt) even worse off than unsecured creditors in a bankruptcy?*

Bankruptcy Code § 510. See also CMBS, Mezzanine Debt, Second Lien Lending, Securitization, Subordination, Subordination Agreement.

## Abandonment

The relinquishment by the bankruptcy estate of any claim to an asset, thus relegating the asset once again to the realm of state law. The sometimes used phrase "abandoned to the secured creditor" is a misnomer. The asset is actually abandoned to the debtor subject to the claims of creditors. Generally, property that is abandoned is abandoned because it is burdensome to the bankruptcy estate or of inconsequential value.

Bankruptcy Code § 554.

## Absolute Assignment of Rents

An assignment of rents where the assignment is treated as a full, complete and absolute transfer of all of the borrower's interest in rents. In contrast, under an assignment of rents for security, the assignment is treated not as absolute but, instead, as creating a lien on the rents in the lender's favor. The most serious consequence to the debtor of characterization of an assignment of rents as "absolute" is that the rents belong to the lender, not the debtor, and may not be used by the debtor as cash collateral or otherwise.

Bankruptcy Code § 363. See also Assignment of Rents, Assignment of Rents for Security, *Butner* Case, Cash Collateral, Use of Cash Collateral.

## Absolute Priority Rule

The Hammer of the (Unsecured Creditor) Gods.

This rule requires that the bankruptcy plan, with respect to each class of unsecured claims that rejects the plan, provide either (1) for payment in full of that class or (2) that classes junior to the rejecting unsecured class will not receive or retain any property (including equity interests in the debtor) under the plan. Generally, a class of unsecured creditors can block a plan that allows the debtor's existing equity holders to retain any property under the plan (including an interest in the reorganized debtor) "on account of" their pre-bankruptcy equity interests unless the plan provides for full payment of unsecured creditors. The rule is an especially powerful weapon in the hands of an undersecured lender because its deficiency claim is likely to dominate the unsecured creditor class in most single asset real estate bankruptcies.

Bankruptcy Code § 1129(b)(2)(B). See also Gerrymandering, *LaSalle* Auction Plan, *LaSalle*, New Value Plan, Non-Impairment Plan, One-Impaired-Class-Must-Accept-The-Plan Rule.

## Acceleration (Reversal Of)

Acceleration of the amount of a debt due to a default under the loan documents can be reversed under certain circumstances (including the curing of the default) without the creditor's claim being considered impaired. A creditor that is not impaired does not have the right to vote on a plan. If a plan impairs no class of creditors, it need not satisfy the One-Impaired-Class-Must -Accept-The-Plan Rule.

Bankruptcy Code § 1124. See also Non-Impairment Plan, One-Impaired-Class-Must-Accept-The-Plan Rule.

## Acceptance of Plan

A vote in favor of a Chapter 11 plan.

Bankruptcy Code § 1126. See also Rejection of Plan.

## Accepting Class

A class of creditors that has voted to accept a plan. A class of creditors has accepted a plan if, with respect to those creditors that voted, creditors that hold at least two-thirds in amount and more than one-half in number of the allowed claims of that class vote to accept the plan.

Bankruptcy Code § 1126. See also One-Impaired-Class-Must-Accept-The-Plan Rule.

## Additional Lien

Granting a lien on some part of the debtor's property in addition to the creditor's existing liens—one of the methods specified in the Code of providing adequate protection to a secured creditor whose collateral may decrease in value because of the automatic stay, the debtor' use, sale, or lease of the property, or any grant of a lien to another creditor under Section 364.

Bankruptcy Code § 361. See also Adequate Protection.

## Adequate Assurance

Protection that must be provided to one who is a party to a lease or contract with the debtor where the debtor is in default under the lease or contract and seeks to *assume* the lease or contract. Even if the debtor is not in default, adequate assurance of future performance must be provided in connection with an *assignment* of the contract or lease.

In the known world always found to be present, never absent.

Bankruptcy Code § 365(c). See also Assumption and Assignment of Executory Contracts and Unexpired Leases, Credit Bid Rights, Shopping Center Lease Provisions.

## Adequate Information

Information that would enable an investor typical of the holders of claims or interests in the case to make an informed judgment about a Chapter 11 plan.

Acceptance or rejection of a plan may not be solicited after the commencement of the case unless the creditor being solicited first receives a copy of the plan or summary of the plan and a written disclosure statement approved by the bankruptcy court as containing "adequate information." In determining the adequacy of the information, the court considers the complexity of the case and the benefit and cost of providing additional information.

Bankruptcy Code § 1125. See also Disclosure Statement

## Adequate Protection

Protection of a secured lender, required by the Code, for any diminution in the value of its collateral in the course of a bankruptcy case resulting from the debtor's use, sale or lease of the property, or any grant of a lien to another creditor under Section 364. May be provided by the making of cash payments to the lender in an amount equivalent to such diminution, by the grant of an additional or replacement lien of a value equivalent to such diminution, or by providing the secured lender with other relief that results in the lender realizing the "indubitable equivalent" of the amount of the diminution in the value of its collateral.

Bankruptcy Code § 361. See also Automatic Stay, Relief From Stay, Replacement Lien, Reverse Alchemy.

## Administrative Consolidation

Consolidation of the administration of the bankruptcy estates of two or more related debtors to reduce the costs of administration and conserve judicial and clerical time. The estates remain separate for the purposes of identifying the assets and liabilities of the separate debtors and determining the dividend to be paid to creditors. Bankruptcy Rule 1015(b) authorizes the bankruptcy court to order the joint administration of cases of two or more debtors if the debtors are (1) a husband and wife, (2) a partnership and one or more of its general partners, (3) two or more general partners of a partnership, or (4) a debtor and its affiliate.

Administrative consolidation is to be contrasted with substantive consolidation of debtors' bankruptcy estates where multiple bankruptcy estates are treated as one entity and the assets and liabilities of each entity are treated as belonging to that single entity.

See also Substantive Consolidation.

## Administrative Convenience Class

A class of claims under a Chapter 11 plan consisting of unsecured claims that are less than (or voluntarily reduced by the claimholder to) a relatively small amount. The amount is subject to bankruptcy court approval on a showing by the plan proponent that the amount designated in the plan is reasonable and necessary for administrative convenience. Often the convenience achieved is the payment in full of the claims in the administrative convenience class on the effective date of the plan or shortly after the effective date, thereby eliminating the expense of making payments over time on numerous small claims.

Debtors sometimes impair an administrative convenience class in an attempt to satisfy the One-Impaired-Class-Must-Accept-The-Plan Rule, but the courts have been unreceptive to that idea, finding that impairment of an administrative convenience class constitutes impermissible gerrymandering designed to improperly "manufacture" an impaired accepting class.

Bankruptcy Code §§ 1122(b), 1129(a)(10). See also Classification of Claims, Cramdown, Gerrymandering, One-Impaired-Class-Must-Accept-The-Plan Rule.

## Administrative Expense

An expense incurred after a case is commenced for the actual and necessary expenses of preserving the bankruptcy estate. Section 503(b) sets forth general but nonexclusive types of expenses that can be allowed administrative expense status, including professionals' compensation and reimbursement of fees and expenses, taxes incurred by the bankruptcy estate, and goods received by the debtor within 20 days of the petition date. An administrative expense has priority in order of payment over general unsecured claims and other priority claims but is not superior to secured claims.

Bankruptcy Code §§ 503, 507(b)(2).

## Administratively Insolvent

Describes a bankruptcy estate that lacks sufficient assets to pay in full the expenses and obligations incurred by the debtor during its Chapter 11 case. Where the debtor's estate is administratively insolvent, postpetition creditors will not be paid in full and prepetition general unsecured creditors will not be paid at all.

Bankruptcy Code §§ 503, 507(b)(1). See also Insolvent.

## Adversary Action

A lawsuit filed in the bankruptcy court, governed generally by the same rules and procedures that apply to a lawsuit filed in a federal district court.

## Affiliate

One type of "insider," whose transactions with a debtor are subject to heightened scrutiny by the bankruptcy courts. Affiliates of a debtor include:

- Persons and entities owning 20 percent or more of the ownership interests in the debtor.

- Entities 20 percent or more of whose voting securities are directly or indirectly controlled by the debtor.

- Persons or entities that operate their businesses under leases or operating agreements with the debtor.

- Persons or entities that operate all or substantially all of the debtor's property under a lease or operating agreement.

- Bankruptcy Code § 101(2). See also Equitable Subordination, Insider, One-Impaired-Class-Must-Accept-The-Plan Rule.

## After-Acquired Property Clause

A security agreement provision granting a security interest in property to be acquired by the debtor in the future.

Section 552 terminates the after-acquired property clause as of the bankruptcy filing. But if the security agreement extends to proceeds, products, offspring, or profits of the collateral, the security interest continues in those items unless the court orders otherwise based on the "equities of the case" (see Equities of the Case). Since the collateral covered by an after-acquired property clause usually constitutes proceeds (see Proceeds), the otherwise potentially devastating consequences of terminating the after-acquired property clause are mitigated. But courts sometimes do not want to extend the proceeds coverage to "secondary" and "tertiary" proceeds (inventory becomes accounts, accounts become cash, cash purchases inventory etc.). The lender usually protects itself from losing its collateral somewhere along the proceeds chain by provisions in cash collateral or DIP financing orders.

Bankruptcy Code § 552. See also Cash Collateral Order, DIP Financing, DIP Financing Order, Equities of the Case, Proceeds.

## After Notice And A Hearing

The right to receive notice of a contemplated action in bankruptcy and the opportunity to be heard. But the right and the notice are sometimes severely curtailed by fast-moving courts and faster-moving debtors that seek relief on an expedited basis (see First Day Motions) at the expense of what a typical non-bankruptcy lawyer might consider fair notice and a meaningful opportunity to be heard.

The Code's definition of "after notice and a hearing" is a dream for any court that loves to freely wield its discretion—"after such notice as is appropriate in the particular circumstances, and such opportunity for a hearing as is appropriate in the particular circumstances." This latitude extends so far as to allow the court to eliminate the opportunity to be heard entirely—if notice is given and "there is insufficient time for a hearing to be commenced before such act must be done, and the court authorizes such action."

Bankruptcy Code § 102(1).

**Alchemy**

The transformation of base metal into gold, such as the creditor's receipt of U.S. Treasury securities in exchange for real estate collateral in a defeasance transaction.

See Defeasance.

But see Reverse Alchemy.

**Allowed Claim**

A claim that is no longer subject to dispute by the debtor or any other party in interest. A claim becomes allowed in the following ways: (1) a proof of claim, upon filing, is deemed allowed unless and until the debtor or a party in interest objects; (2) in Chapter 11 cases, any scheduled claim that is not listed on the debtor's schedules as disputed, contingent, or unliquidated is deemed allowed; (3) a claim that is allowed by the court after an objection is filed and heard is an allowed claim; or (4) a contingent or unliquidated claim that is estimated under Section 502(c) by the court is an allowed claim.

An allowed claim confers a right to distributions (if there are any) and the right to vote on the plan (if the claim is in an impaired class).

Creditors often do not know until very late in a case whether their claims will, in the end, be allowed claims, because debtors and other parties in interest frequently wait until near the close of the bankruptcy case to file objections to claims.

Bankruptcy Code §§ 301, 303. See also Contingent Claim, Disputed Claim, Oversecured Creditor, Undersecured Creditor, Unliquidated Claim, Unsecured Claim.

**Arbitration**

An alternative form of dispute resolution. Contract clauses requiring it are more enforceable in bankruptcy than one who has not read the case law might believe.

**Artificial Impairment**

An impairment of the rights of a class under a Chapter 11 plan that is *de minimis* or proposed with a motive to "manufacture" an impaired class to satisfy the One-Impaired-Class-Must-Accept-The-Plan Rule.

See also Cramdown, Impairment, One-Impaired-Class-Must-Accept-The-Plan Rule.

**Assignment of Executory Contracts and Unexpired Leases**

See Assumption and Assignment of Executory Contracts and Unexpired Leases.

**Assignment of Rents**

An agreement under which the borrower transfers to the lender the borrower's interest in rents generated by the borrower's real property, either absolutely or as security for a debt. Rents are "cash collateral" under the Code, and the lender is entitled to "adequate protection" before the debtor will be allowed to use the rents.

Bankruptcy Code § 363. See also Absolute Assignment of Rents, Adequate Protection, Assignment of Rents for Security, *Butner* Case, Use of Cash Collateral.

## Assignment of Rents for Security

An assignment of rents serving as collateral for a debt, as opposed to an absolute assignment of rents. A split has developed among the courts. Some courts have decided that any assignment that is revocable upon full payment of the debt to the lender is necessarily an assignment "for security" even if the agreement is phrased in absolute assignment language. Other courts have ruled that if an assignment is fashioned as "absolute," with a debtor holding a mere license to collect and make use of rents prior to an event of default, the form of assignment is enforceable, including in bankruptcy. The latter interpretation has resulted in the rents not being property of the estate, severely limiting a Chapter 11 debtor's ability to reorganize.

Bankruptcy Code § 363. See also Absolute Assignment of Rents, Adequate Protection, Assignment of Rents, *Butner* Case, Cash Collateral, Use of Cash Collateral.

## Assumption and Assignment of Executory Contracts and Unexpired Leases

"Assumption" is the debtor's election to bind itself, postpetition, to continue performance of obligations under an executory contract or unexpired lease, including curing defaults as required by the Code. Assumption of an executory contract or unexpired lease is accomplished either through a court order approving the debtor's motion to assume or by confirmation of a Chapter 11 plan providing for the assumption. Assumption enables a debtor to retain in full force those contracts and leases it believes are favorable to it.

Assumption is the opposite of "rejection" of an executory contract or unexpired lease where a debtor opts to no longer perform (see Rejection of Executory Contracts and Unexpired Leases).

Assignment enables a debtor to transfer assumed leases and contracts (subject to certain limitations stated in Section 365). If the debtor breaches an executory contract or unexpired lease after assumption, the damages claim of the non-debtor party to the contract or lease is entitled to administrative expense status.

Bankruptcy Code § 365. See also Adequate Assurance, *Ipso Facto* Clause/Provision, Rejection of Executory Contracts and Unexpired Leases, Shopping Center Lease Provisions.

## Attorneys' Fees

Despised by all except those who receive them. Attorneys' fees for postpetition services, whether incurred by the lender's counsel, debtor's counsel, or a committee's counsel are subject to review by the bankruptcy court for reasonableness, and are payable as an administrative expense. The secured lender's attorneys' fees may be paid from its collateral if the lender is oversecured.

See also Administrative Expense, Oversecured Creditor, Undersecured Creditor.

## Automatic Stay

A statutory injunction, effective immediately upon the filing of a bankruptcy case, prohibiting certain creditor actions against the debtor or the debtor's property. The automatic stay is designed to provide the debtor a "breathing spell" after the bankruptcy filing. Creditors are allowed to seek relief from the stay.

Bankruptcy Code § 362. See also Motion for Relief from Stay, Stay Relief.

**Avoidance Action**

A lawsuit filed by the debtor or other estate representative seeking to "avoid" (nullify) certain transfers made by the debtor. Fraudulent transfer actions and preference actions are forms of avoidance actions as are certain exercises of the strong arm powers under Section 544 and actions to avoid certain postpetition transfers under Section 549.

Bankruptcy Code §§ 544-550. See also Fraudulent Transfer, Preference, Strong Arm Powers.

**Bad Faith Filing**

The commencement of a bankruptcy case for an improper motive including a filing that is inconsistent with the principles and purposes of the Code.

The following have been considered to be hallmarks of a bad faith Chapter 11 filing: (1) the bankruptcy filing was prompted by what is essentially a two party dispute between the debtor and another person or entity; (2) the debtor is solvent or has relatively few unsecured creditors or little unsecured debt, which it is able to pay; (3) the appearance of forum shopping in filing the bankruptcy case; and (4) the petition was filed to delay legitimate enforcement rights of a creditor without any intent to reorganize.

Bankruptcy Code § 1112. See also Dismissal.

## Bankruptcy Code

Refers to Title 11 of the United States Code, 11 U.S.C. §§ 101-1532, which governs all bankruptcy cases filed since October 1, 1979. Often referred to simply as "the Code."

## Bankruptcy Estate

The estate created upon the filing of a bankruptcy petition, consisting of all of the debtor's property rights and interests.

Bankruptcy Code § 541. See also Property of the Estate.

## Bankruptcy Petition

The document filed by the debtor to initiate its bankruptcy case.

Bankruptcy Code § 301. See also Involuntary Bankruptcy Petition, Order for Relief, Voluntary Bankruptcy Petition.

## Bankruptcy Proof

A delusion. The idea that contractual provisions, perhaps combined with a structural device such as an "independent" director with veto power over a bankruptcy filing, can absolutely *prevent* a debtor from filing a bankruptcy case because the debtor is now "bankruptcy proof." This is a delusion. The courts are likely to strike down such contractual provisions and structural devices if they too directly

23

prevent or somehow make it virtually impossible to file a bankruptcy case. But provisions designed to make a bankruptcy more "remote" are more likely to be upheld. See Special (or Single) Purpose Bankruptcy Remote Entity.

See also Independent Director, Special (or Single) Purpose Bankruptcy Remote Entity.

## Bankruptcy Remote

See Special (or Single) Purpose Bankruptcy Remote Entity.

## Bankruptcy Rules

See Federal Rules of Bankruptcy Procedure.

## Bankruptcy Trustee

See Chapter 7 Trustee, Chapter 11 Trustee.

## BAPCA

The Bankruptcy Abuse Prevention and Consumer Protection Act of 2005. A series of creditor-friendly and debtor-hostile amendments to the Bankruptcy Code passed by Congress in April of 2005 and generally effective starting October 17, 2005.

To creditors, an eminently sensible piece of legislation that eliminated various debtor excesses. To debtors, the modern day version of debtors' prisons.

See Thermidorean Reaction.

## Bar Date

A deadline set by the bankruptcy court for creditors to file proofs of claim against the debtor's estate.

See also Proof of Claim.

## Best Interest of Creditors Test

The requirement under the Code that *each creditor* that has not accepted a Chapter 11 plan must receive under the plan no less than it would receive if the debtor's assets were liquidated in a Chapter 7 case.

Bankruptcy Code § 1129(a)(7). See also Confirmation Requirements.

## *BFP* Case

United States Supreme Court case holding that the price received from a high bidder at a regularly conducted foreclosure sale of real estate held in accordance with applicable state law conclusively establishes "reasonably equivalent value" and, therefore, prevents such a sale from being a constructively fraudulent transfer.

The court in *BFP* affirmed the lower courts' rulings that the sale could not constitute a fraudulent transfer under Section 548 even though the amount bid at the sale was $433,000 and there was evidence that the property was worth $725,000 at the time of the sale. The court also criticized the holdings of *Durrett* and similar cases, which had compared the sale price at foreclosure to a property's "fair market value" in determining whether a foreclosure bid price constituted "reasonably equivalent value."

The *BFP* holding does not extent to personal property foreclosures under the UCC, as the court emphasized that its decision applied only to real estate mortgage foreclosures and noted that considerations relating to other forced sales may be different.

Bankruptcy Code § 548. See also *Durrett* Case, Constructively Fraudulent Transfer, Reasonably Equivalent Value.

## Bid Protections

Safeguards for a buyer that enters into an agreement to purchase assets of the debtor in a 363 sale.

In almost all 363 sales the debtor will negotiate a purchase agreement with provisions in the agreement allowing other potential purchasers to submit higher or better bids. The purchaser that negotiates the purchase agreement, often referred to as the "stalking horse," invests its time and money in developing and negotiating the agreement as well as for due diligence. As a means of protecting its interests and covering the expenses it incurs for due diligence and in negotiating the purchase agreement, the stalking horse will typically demand that other offers for the debtor's assets meet certain requirements. For example, the stalking horse will typically insist on a break-up fee and that offers from other prospective purchasers include terms substantially similar to the terms stated in the purchase agreement between the stalking horse and the debtor.

See also 363 Auction, 363 Sale, Break-Up Fee, Sale Free and Clear, Stalking Horse, Topping Fee.

## Bona Fide Dispute

If certain conditions are satisfied, the debtor may sell assets free and clear of existing liens and other interests, with any liens or interests attaching to the proceeds of the sale. One of the situations where this is permitted is when a lien or interest is "in bona fide dispute." A bona fide dispute is one that is backed by a good faith, colorable argument.

Bankruptcy Code § 363(f)(4). See also 363 Auction, 363 Sale, Sale Free and Clear.

## Bona Fide Purchaser

A purchaser that acquires property without "notice" of any outstanding claims held against the property by third parties and that gives value for the property. "Notice" includes actual notice, notice of facts that should have triggered further inquiry by the purchaser, and constructive notice.

The trustee (and, therefore, the debtor in possession) has the powers of a *bona fide* purchaser of real property and may avoid the transfer of property or an obligation incurred by the debtor (including liens against the debtor's property) that would be voidable by a purchaser of *real* property that obtained and perfected its status as a *bona fide* purchaser as of the time of the bankruptcy filing.

Bankruptcy Code § 544(a)(3). See also Avoidance Actions, Hypothetical Lien Creditor, Strong Arm Powers.

**Break-Up Fee**

A fee paid to the stalking horse from the proceeds of a 363 sale if it is not the successful bidder. The fee has been justified on various grounds, including compensation to the stalking horse for adding value for jump-starting the sale process by entering into a purchase agreement. May also be paid to compensate the stalking horse for its time and expense incurred in connection with negotiating the terms of the sale and conducting its due diligence.

See also 363 Auction, 363 Sale, Asset Sale, Bid Protections, Stalking Horse.

***Butner* Case**

The United States Supreme Court case where the Court made clear that property interests are created and defined by state law and that determination of property rights in bankruptcy is generally a matter of state law. In *Butner*, the mortgagee under a real property mortgage had failed to take the steps necessary to enforce its potential interest in rents generated by the property prior to the debtor's bankruptcy filing. The lender then failed to follow up during the bankruptcy case with any appropriate action to gain possession of the rents.

The Supreme Court found that the Code does not make a lender's interest or potential interest in rents under a mortgage automatically effective. Instead,

the Court emphasized that in cases where a lender's right in rents had not been made effective under state law prior to the bankruptcy filing, a lender must take affirmative action *during the bankruptcy case* equivalent to the action required under state law to gain possession of the rents (such as obtaining stay relief and immediately foreclosing, or filing a motion to sequester rents). The Court in *Butner* did not specify the actions required of a lender in any given case, leaving that determination instead to the lower courts and their greater familiarity with the state law requisites for a lender's enforcement of interests in rents generated by their collateral.

See also, Absolute Assignment of Rents, Assignment of Rents, Assignment of Rents for Security.

## Call Protection

See Default Prepayment Clause, Defeasance, Prepayment Consideration, Prepayment Penalty, Prepayment Premium, Yield Maintenance.

## Carveout

The agreement of a lender to make advances or set aside ("carve out") some of its collateral to pay the fees of debtor's counsel and financial advisors, and counsel and financial advisors to a committee. The carveout is often seen as the "toll" the lender must pay to use the bankruptcy estate to obtain a more profitable liquidation of its collateral. The terms of a carveout are usually negotiated in connection with a DIP financing agreement or cash collateral order.

Bankruptcy Code § 506(c). See also Cash Collateral Order, DIP Financing Order, Surcharge. And for a very different kind of "carveout," see Nonrecourse Carveout.

## Cash Collateral

The debtor's cash, the lender's collateral. Cash (or cash equivalents) in which the debtor has an interest and that is subject to a lender's lien. The debtor may use cash collateral only if the lender consents or if the court, after a contested hearing, finds that the lender's collateral position is adequately protected.

Bankruptcy Code § 363(a). See also Adequate Protection, Cash Collateral Order, Use of Cash Collateral.

## Cash Collateral Order

Order of the bankruptcy court that governs the conditions of the debtor's use of the lender's cash collateral. The cash collateral order is usually entered at the outset of the case, either after an agreement between the borrower and lender or after a hotly contested hearing at which the lender and debtor argue about whether the lender's interest in the cash is adequately protected or whether the cash is property of the debtor at all.

In those instances where the lender and debtor agree to the terms of a cash collateral order, the lender often is able to extract from the debtor a number of pro-lender concessions.

Bankruptcy Code § 363(c)(2). See also Adequate Protection, Cash Collateral, Use of Cash Collateral.

## CDO

See Collateralized Debt Obligation.

## Chapter 7

Chapter of the Code that provides for a trustee to take control of the debtor's property, to sell or dispose of it, and to distribute the proceeds to creditors in accordance with the distribution provisions of the Code. The association of the concept of liquidation exclusively with Chapter 7 is misleading because under current Chapter 11 practice many plans actually implement a liquidation instead of a reorganization.

See also Chapter 7 Trustee.

## Chapter 7 Trustee

A person appointed in a Chapter 7 case to liquidate the debtor's assets and distribute any proceeds to creditors. The Chapter 7 trustee—rather than the debtor—controls and administers all property of the bankruptcy estate. Unlike in Chapter 11, there is a trustee appointed in every Chapter 7 case.

Bankruptcy Code §§ 701-704. See also Chapter 11 Trustee.

## Chapter 9

Chapter of the Code that governs adjustment of debts of municipalities.

Bankruptcy Code §§ 901-946.

## Chapter 11

Chapter of the Code that governs reorganization of debts of business entities and individuals not eligible to reorganize under Chapter 13 (see Chapter 13). Chapter 11 allows the debtor to attempt to reorganize its financial affairs or liquidate its assets under a

Chapter 11 plan. Under Chapter 11, the debtor typically remains in possession of its assets, but the court under certain conditions can displace the debtor in possession with a Chapter 11 trustee.

Bankruptcy Code §§ 1101-1146.

## Chapter 11 Plan

A document proposing the terms for reorganizing or liquidating the debtor's business.

The plan is usually filed by the debtor but is sometimes filed by creditors or other parties in interest. If confirmed, the plan governs the debtor's rights and obligations when it emerges from bankruptcy. The plan is treated as a contract between the debtor and its creditors governing their post-confirmation relationships. A plan will sometimes not envision a debtor's reorganization or emergence from bankruptcy at all but may instead provide for liquidation of the debtor's assets.

Bankruptcy Code §§ 1121-1129. See also Competing Plan, Confirmation Requirements, Liquidating Plan.

## Chapter 11 Trustee

A trustee appointed by the bankruptcy court to take control of the debtor's assets in a Chapter 11 case.

The debtor is entitled to remain in possession and control of its property unless a Chapter 11 trustee is appointed or the case is converted to Chapter 7. A Chapter 11 trustee may be appointed if the debtor is guilty of fraud, dishonesty, mismanagement, or incompetence, or if appointment of a trustee would be in the best interests of creditors, equity holders, and other interests of the bankruptcy estate. The Chapter 11 trustee has the responsibility for the operation of the business and the formulation of a

Chapter 11 plan. Only a clear showing of improper conduct by the debtor, impending disaster, or other substantial "cause" will persuade the court to appoint a Chapter 11 trustee.

Bankruptcy Code § 1104. See also Examiner.

**Chapter 12**

Chapter of the Code that governs adjustment of the debts of a family farmer with regular annual income.

Bankruptcy Code §§ 1201-1231.

**Chapter 13**

Chapter of the Code that governs the adjustment of debts of an individual with regular income.

Chapter 13 allows an individual meeting certain qualifications, including a regular income and debt not exceeding certain dollar amounts, to pay that individual's debts, or a portion of those debts, over time from future income (rather than having all of the debtor's non-exempt assets liquidated as would occur in a Chapter 7 case). Chapter 13 is not available to a corporate or partnership debtor. If an individual debtor is not eligible to use Chapter 13 because the debtor's debts exceed the limits applicable to Chapter 13 cases, the debtor may use Chapter 11 to reorganize.

Bankruptcy Code §§ 1301-1330.

**Chapter 22**

Term used to describe a second Chapter 11 filing by a debtor that has been through a Chapter 11 case previously. The existence of a "Chapter 22" is especially prevalent among large debtors and is thought by some to be the consequence of the bankruptcy courts essentially deferring to the debtor and its advisors in the first bankruptcy case, leaving the real job of reorganization unfinished. Chapter 33 refers to the third Chapter 11, Chapter 44 the fourth, etc.

*Synonyms: Dracula's Daughters, The Undead (to grant them eternal rest the lender's lawyer must devise a creditors' rights equivalent of a stake in the heart, garlic in the mouth, and a crucifix on the forehead).*

See also Lopucki.

## Claim

The right to payment, whether or not that right is reduced to judgment, liquidated, unliquidated, fixed, contingent, matured, unmatured, disputed, undisputed, legal, equitable, secured or unsecured. A claim also includes the right to an equitable remedy for breach of performance if such breach gives rise to a right of payment.

Bankruptcy Code § 101(5).

## Claims Trading

The purchase and sale of bankruptcy claims.

## Classification of Claims

Grouping of claims into classes under a Chapter 11 plan.

Bankruptcy Code § 1122. See also Confirmation Requirements, Gerrymandering, One-Impaired-Class-Must-Accept-The-Plan Rule.

## CMBS

See Commercial Mortgage Backed Securities, Securitization.

## Code

Informal name for the Bankruptcy Code.

**Co-Debtor**

A party who is jointly liable with another on a debt or liability. Although the Code states that the discharge of the debtor does not result in a discharge of a guarantor or other co-debtor, Chapter 11 plans often include injunctions against prosecution of claims against co-debtors, which the courts sometimes uphold and sometimes strike down.

Bankruptcy Code § 524(e). See also Subrogation Rights, Surety.

**Coerced Loan Approach**

One of the methods the bankruptcy courts use to set the cramdown interest rate that a plan must provide to a secured creditor that does not accept the plan. Under the coerced loan approach (also referred to as the "forced loan approach"), the court sets the cramdown interest rate at the rate that the creditor would receive if the creditor were permitted to liquidate its collateral and reinvest the proceeds in a new loan to a third party (free of any coercion), on terms comparable to the "forced loan" under the debtor's plan in terms of duration and risk. The coerced loan approach is one species of the "market rate approach" (see Market Rate Approach), and was rejected by the United States Supreme Court (see Cramdown Interest Rate) in favor of the formula approach (see Formula Approach).

See also Cost of Funds Approach, Cramdown, Cramdown Interest Rate, Forced Loan Approach, Formula Approach, Market Rate Approach, Presumptive Contract Rate Approach, Prime Plus Formula Approach, Treasury Plus Formula Approach.

## Collateralized Debt Obligation

A securitization of debt obligations. A highly addictive financing tool for lenders, it has been around in the commercial lending arena for some time (also referred to a CLO (Collateralized Loan Obligation)). This Kool Aid only recently trickled into the real estate lending water supply. Used originally by specialty finance lenders, then by investment banks, it is now being employed by some of the nation's largest commercial banks, and, as of this writing in early 2007, the real estate lending community is gulping it down in a gluttonous frenzy.

Much more flexible and user-friendly than a REMIC (see REMIC), this technique (or "technology," as in "CDO technology," as its buzzword-wielding practitioners like to refer to it) is replacing so-called "large loan" REMIC securitizations and includes so-called "transitional" debt instruments (such as short-term bridge loans), mezzanine debt, and other debt mostly of a shorter term and floating rate nature.

If the financial wizards figure out how to plug this technology into a "true sale" format or otherwise how to remove the loans from the balance sheet of the original lender (already the equity in the CDO's is being sold, thus removing the asset from the originator's balance sheet), REMIC-based CMBS may go the way of the Dodo.

These are put together with the typical rating agency fanatical focus on "bankruptcy remoteness," but some of these lender/debtors could end up in their own Chapter 11 cases, trying to evade "bankruptcy remoteness" in their own bankruptcies while enforcing it in their borrowers' cases.

See also Commercial Mortgage Backed Securities, REMIC, Securitization, Special (or Single) Purpose Bankruptcy Remote Entity.

## Collective Bargaining Agreement

Labor agreements that are theoretically more difficult to reject than normal contracts, but as Northwest's employees and other union employees have learned, these agreements can not only be rejected but the employees can be deprived of the right to strike following rejection.

Bankruptcy Code § 1113. See also Executory Contract, Assumption and Assignment of Executory Contracts and Unexpired Leases, Rejection of Executory Contracts and Unexpired Leases.

## Collusive Bidding

A secret agreement among bidders or potential bidders to manipulate the price paid for property at a 363 sale. Collusive bidding may subject the colluding parties to criminal liability.

## Commercial Mortgage Backed Securities

See Securitization.

## Committee

See Creditors' Committee.

## Competing Plan

A plan that is in competition with another plan filed in a debtor's Chapter 11 case. A non-debtor proponent is required to wait until after the debtor's period of exclusivity has expired before filing a competing plan. The competing plan can be an effective secured creditor tactic often superior to a stay relief motion.

Bankruptcy Code §§ 1121(c), 1129(c). See also Exclusivity Period.

## Confirmation

Formal court approval of a bankruptcy plan, with the result that the plan becomes binding on creditors and other parties affected by the plan. "Confirmation" is a glorious term to the reorganizing debtor if it is the debtor's plan being confirmed and a less than glorious term if the plan being confirmed is a completing plan or a liquidating plan.

Bankruptcy Code § 1129. See also Confirmation Hearing, Confirmation Order, Confirmation Requirements.

## Confirmation Hearing

The day of reckoning for the debtor. At this hearing the court decides whether to approve a bankruptcy plan. Other critical events—such as valuation of the debtor's property and determination of a secured creditor's right to relief from the automatic stay—often coincide with the confirmation hearing.

Bankruptcy Code § 1129. See also Confirmation, Confirmation Order, Confirmation Requirements.

## Confirmation Order

The bankruptcy court's order confirming a Chapter 11 plan.

See also Confirmation, Confirmation Hearing, Confirmation Requirements.

## Confirmation Requirements

The requirements, set out in Section 1129, that a plan proponent must satisfy to obtain confirmation of its Chapter 11 plan. One of those requirements is the do-or-die requirement that if any class is impaired under the plan (see Impaired Class), at least one impaired class must accept the plan by two-thirds in amount and a majority in number of those voting (see One-Impaired-Class-Must-Accept-The-Plan Rule). The proponent must also show, among other things, that:

- The plan is feasible (see Feasibility Test).

- Creditors will receive under the plan at least as much as they would receive if the debtor's assets were liquidated under Chapter 7 (see Best Interest of Creditors Test).

If any impaired class does not accept the plan (see Accepting Class), the proponent of the plan can ask the court for a "cramdown" of the plan on the non-accepting classes (see Cramdown). A successful cramdown, however, requires a showing that the plan:

- Is fair and equitable to any non-accepting impaired class (see Fair and Equitable Test).

- Does not unfairly discriminate against any non-accepting impaired class (see Unfair Discrimination).

- Does not violate the absolute priority rule (see Absolute Priority Rule).

Bankruptcy Code § 1129. See also Absolute Priority Rule, Best Interest of Creditors Test, Chapter 11 Plan, Confirmation, Confirmation Order, Cramdown Interest Rate, Fair and Equitable Test, Feasibility Test, Impaired Class, One-Impaired-Class-Must-Accept-The-Plan Rule.

## Conflicts Counsel

Counsel retained to represent a trustee, debtor, or committee in a matter where primary counsel has a conflict of interest.

## Constructively Fraudulent Transfer

A transfer of a property interest by a debtor that is avoidable—not on account of actual fraudulent intent—but because the debtor made a transfer in exchange for less than reasonably equivalent value. Such a transfer is avoidable if the debtor can show that at the time of the transfer it was insolvent or that the transfer rendered the debtor insolvent.

Fraudulent transfers occurring within two years prior to the bankruptcy filing are avoidable under Section 548 in bankruptcy cases filed on or after October 17, 2006 (or within one year in bankruptcy cases filed before October 17, 2006). State laws on fraudulent transfers utilize longer reach-back periods than two years (typically, four years) and can be used by estate representatives under some circumstances under Section 544.

Bankruptcy Code §§ 544, 548(a)(1)(B). See also Avoidance Action, Intentionally Fraudulent Transfer, Strong Arm Powers.

## Contemporaneous Exchange for New Value Defense

One of the defenses available to a creditor in a preference action. The defense requires a showing that the creditor gave new value to the debtor in exchange for the allegedly preferential transfer and that the creditor gave the value to the debtor at substantially the same time that the debtor made its transfer to the creditor.

Bankruptcy Code § 547(c)(1). See also Ordinary Course Defense, Preference.

## Contested Matter

A proceeding in a bankruptcy case created when a party files a motion asking for relief from the bankruptcy court, as compared to an "adversary proceeding" created when a party files a complaint.

Contested matters differ from adversary proceedings primarily in the procedures employed by the court. A contested matter is generally less formal and is heard more quickly than an adversary proceeding. Another difference is that adversary actions sometimes involve jury trial rights while contested matters do not.

Stay relief motions, motions for valuation, and motions to assume or reject unexpired leases or executory contracts, for example, all give rise to contested matters. Preference lawsuits, fraudulent transfer lawsuits, and avoidance actions under Section 544 are examples of adversary actions.

See also Adversary Action.

## Contingent Claim

A claim upon which a debtor may be liable to pay upon the occurrence of a future event or circumstance. The most common contingent claim is a claim on a guaranty when the obligation guaranteed is not in default.

Bankruptcy Code § 502(c). See also Estimation of Claims, Unliquidated Claim.

## Contract Rate

The rate of interest specified in a promissory note or other contract.

See also Cramdown Interest Rate, Single Asset Real Estate.

## Conversion

Usually, for a debtor, something far less than a "religious" experience.

The changing of a bankruptcy case from one chapter to another, sometimes at the debtor's request or with the debtor's consent, other times not. A conversion without the debtor's consent is normally the result of an ineffective or plodding reorganization effort, leading a creditor or other party in interest to ask the court to convert a Chapter 11 case into a Chapter 7 case so that the debtor's assets are promptly liquidated to prevent further erosion in the value of the assets of the bankruptcy estate.

Bankruptcy Code §§ 706, 1112.

**Co-Obligor**

See Co-Debtor.

**Cost of Funds Approach**

A method rarely but occasionally employed by some bankruptcy courts to set the cramdown interest rate. This approach sets the cramdown interest rate at a rate that approximates the creditor's cost to borrow funds in the marketplace. Some courts then add a risk premium to that rate to arrive at the cramdown interest rate. The United States Supreme Court's decision in the *Till* case makes it unlikely that any bankruptcy court would continue to use the cost of funds approach.

See also Coerced Loan Approach, Cramdown Interest Rate, Forced Loan Approach, Formula Approach, Market Rate Approach, Presumptive Contract Rate Approach, Prime Plus Formula Approach, Treasury Plus Formula Approach.

**Cramdown**

The effort by a debtor to obtain plan confirmation over the objection of an impaired, non-accepting class of creditors ("cramming the plan down the creditor's throat").

Often incorrectly used to describe the reduction in amount of a secured claim by operation of Section 506(b), which grants the creditor a secured claim only to the extent of the value of its collateral.

A cramdown usually involves an effort by the debtor to confirm a plan that reduces the lender's interest rate, changes the amortization schedule of the lender's loan, extends the maturity date of the loan, or otherwise changes the lender's rights.

A plan cannot be crammed down if it unfairly discriminates against a class that did not accept the plan and unless the plan is fair and equitable to each class that did not accept the plan.

Bankruptcy Code § 1129(b). See Confirmation Requirements, Cramdown Interest Rate, Fair and Equitable Test, Gerrymandering, Indubitable Equivalent, Unfair Discrimination.

## Cramdown Interest Rate

The rate of interest forced on a secured creditor under a Chapter 11 plan that is confirmed over the creditor's objection.

The court has the power to confirm a reorganizing plan over the objection of an impaired class of secured creditors (a "cramdown") if the plan meets certain requirements. One of the requirements for a successful cramdown is that the debtor prove that the payments to the lender on its secured claim have a present value (as of the effective date of the plan) of at least the amount of the secured claim. If the debtor and creditor cannot agree on an interest rate, then the court must decide in connection with the confirmation hearing what rate of interest would be appropriate. The court's determination of the cramdown interest rate usually involves a battle between expert witnesses for the debtor and the objecting secured creditor.

Courts have used a variety of approaches to determine the appropriate cramdown interest rate, including the formula approach, the prime plus formula approach, the treasury plus formula approach, the coerced loan approach (often called the forced loan approach), the cost of funds approach and the presumptive contract rate approach.

As a result of the decision of the United States Supreme Court in *Till v. SCS Credit Corporation*, the most likely approach that a bankruptcy court will use in any given case is the formula approach. (see Formula Approach). But the decision in the *Till* case is not entirely clear, and it is possible that a court in any given case might use any of the approaches mentioned above (or a variant of one of those approaches) to determine the cramdown interest rate.

Bankruptcy Code § 1129(b)(2)(A)(ii). See also Coerced Loan Approach, Cost of Funds Approach, Cramdown, Forced Loan Approach, Formula Approach, Market Rate Approach, Presumptive Contract Rate Approach, Prime Plus Formula Approach, Treasury Plus Formula Approach.

## Credit Bid Rights

A secured creditor's right to bid at any sale of its collateral by bidding up to the amount of its debt without having to pay cash. Unless the court orders otherwise, a secured creditor is allowed to credit bid at any sale of its collateral.

Bankruptcy Code § 363(k). See 363 Auction, 363 Sale.

## Creditors' Committee

A group of unsecured creditors appointed by the United States Trustee charged with being a watchdog to protect the interests of similarly situated creditors in a bankruptcy case.

Usually consists of five to seven creditors chosen from the 20 largest unsecured creditors in the case. Although the term is normally used to refer to the official committee of unsecured creditors, other committees often exist in bankruptcy cases, such as bondholders committees, employee and retiree committees, and equity holders committees.

Committees are represented by counsel at the expense of the bankruptcy estate and often at the expense of secured creditors—sometimes with, and sometimes without, their consent.

Bankruptcy Code §§ 705, 1102, 1103. See also Carveout, Creditors' Committee, Equity Holders' Committee, Retirees' Committee, Surcharge.

## Critical Vendors

A group of prepetition vendors that the debtor asserts are so vital to the debtor's operations that payment of their claims at or near the beginning of the debtor's Chapter 11 case is justified—a huge advantage to those vendors if the court agrees with the debtor's position because normally the debtor cannot pay prepetition claims until after confirmation of its Chapter 11 plan.

*Synonym: Fortunate Sons.*

See also Doctrine of Necessity.

## Cross-Collateralization

Taking a security interest in collateral to secure multiple loans. Condemned by the courts if directly securing prepetition debt with postpetition collateral in cash collateral and financing orders but usually allowed if indirectly accomplished by extending a new loan postpetition that pays the prepetition loan in full.

See also Cash Collateral Order, DIP Financing, Roll-Over.

## Custodian

A person in possession of the debtor's property, usually a receiver appointed by a state court before the debtor's bankruptcy case was filed.

The Code requires a custodian to turn over the debtor's property to the debtor upon the debtor's bankruptcy filing. But the bankruptcy court may leave the custodian in possession if it determines that doing so would serve the best interests of creditors.

When bankruptcy is imminent, the secured creditor often races to the courthouse to obtain the appointment of a receiver, hoping that the court will continue the receiver in possession post-bankruptcy.

Bankruptcy Code §§ 101(11), 543. See also Property of the Estate, Turnover.

## Debtor

A person or entity in bankruptcy. Not every person or entity is eligible to file a bankruptcy case under every Chapter of the Code; for example, only persons and entities that reside, have a domicile, or have a place of business or have property in the United States are eligible for relief under the Code.

Bankruptcy Code §§ 101(13), 109.

## Debtor In Possession

A Chapter 11 debtor that remains in possession of its property and operates its business after commencing a Chapter 11 case. Often referred to as the D-I-P (pronouncing each letter). Appointment of a Chapter 11 Trustee reduces a debtor in possession to a mere "debtor."

In Chapter 11 cases where the debtor remains in possession, the debtor (with minor exceptions) has the rights, powers, and functions of a trustee appointed under the Code. The Code often references only the rights and functions of "the trustee," but in Chapter 11 cases those references should be read as "the trustee or debtor in possession."

Bankruptcy Code § 1107. See also Chapter 11 Trustee, Debtor, DIP.

## Deemed Rejection

The rejection of an executory contract or unexpired lease as a result of the debtor's failure to affirmatively assume or reject the contract or lease within the time specified by the Code.

In Chapter 7 cases an executory contract or unexpired lease of residential real property is deemed rejected if not assumed or rejected by the debtor within 60 days after the order for relief (or within such additional time as the court allows for assumption or rejection).

If the debtor is a lessee under an unexpired lease of nonresidential real property, the lease is deemed rejected if not assumed or rejected by the debtor within the earlier of 120 days after the order for relief (which may be extended by the court for a period not to exceed an additional 90 days) or the entry of an order confirming a plan. In the case of deemed rejection of an unexpired lease of nonresidential real property, the Code offers the landlord an added benefit by requiring that the debtor immediately surrender the property to the lessor.

Bankruptcy Code §§ 365(a), 365(d). See also Assumption and Assignment of Executory Contracts and Unexpired Leases, Executory Contract, Rejection of Executory Contracts and Unexpired Leases, Unexpired Lease.

## Deepening Insolvency

A cause of action recognized in some jurisdictions under which directors, officers and others may be held liable for continuing to operate a business after the business has become insolvent, allowing the business to continue to incur debt and, by doing so, "deepening" the debtor's insolvency.

See also Zone of Insolvency.

## Default Prepayment Clause

A loan document provision requiring the borrower to pay yield maintenance or other call protection when an event of default occurs. Absent this provision, a borrower could deliberately default and escape the lender's call protection.

*Diabolical Questions: Is this provision enforceable in bankruptcy? Can it, with many other provisions, be stripped from the lender by a Chapter 11 plan?*

## Default Rate

An increased interest rate imposed by the lender's loan documents triggered by the borrower's default under the loan documents.

Under Section 506(b), an oversecured lender is entitled to interest on its claim, together with fees, costs, or charges under its loan documents. But the Section explicitly states that fees, costs and charges must be "reasonable," while imposing no such limitation on the oversecured creditor's right to interest. This has led some courts and scholars to debate whether the creditor is entitled to interest at its contract rate—even if it entails the allowance of default interest—or at some other, unspecified rate.

Bankruptcy Code § 506(b). See also Interest, Oversecured Creditor, Secured Claim.

## Defeasance

The substitution of U.S. Treasury or Agency securities for real estate as collateral for a loan in an amount sufficient to pay each scheduled periodic payment and the final balloon payment on the loan so that the loan is paid in full from the new collateral in accordance with the loan's scheduled payment terms.

*Diabolical Questions include: Are defeasance provisions enforceable by specific performance outside of bankruptcy? If so, are they also enforceable by specific performance in a bankruptcy case?*

See also Alchemy, Call Protection, Cramdown, Default Prepayment, Indubitable Equivalent, Yield Maintenance.

## Deficiency Claim

The difference between the court-determined value of the lender's collateral and the amount of the lender's total claim. A deficiency claim that is nonrecourse under the loan documents is transformed into a recourse claim under Chapter 11 (but not Chapter 7) by Section 1111(b)(1). It is the undersecured creditor's "virtual" recourse deficiency claim that often gives it a powerful blocking position with respect to a Chapter 11 plan.

Bankruptcy Code §§ 506(a), 1111(b)(1). See also 1111(b) Election, Alchemy, Confirmation Requirements, Undersecured Creditor.

## *Deprizio* Doctrine

Doctrine that imposed preference liability on a creditor in a most ingenious and unexpected way, by combining provisions of Sections 547 and 550.

In a 1989 United States Supreme Court case, a crafty trustee successfully argued that a debtor's payment of a debt guaranteed by the debtor's insider was made for the benefit of the guarantor/insider because it eliminated a portion of the guarantor's exposure on the guaranty. Accordingly, payments made within one year (the statutory reach-back period applicable to preferences to insiders) of the commencement of the case, and not just within 90 days prior to the case (the period applicable to non-insiders) were avoidable by the trustee under Section 547.

The hook: under Section 550, the preference could be recovered from either the party for whose benefit it was made (i.e., the guarantor) or the party to whom it was made (the lender). This two step approach rendered non-insider lenders liable for payments received by them during the extended reach-back period.

This anomalous result (from the creditor's standpoint, if not from the trustee's) has been cured by Congress, after more than one attempt, but the doctrine nevertheless lurks as a ghost, roaming the corridors of financial institutions, bankruptcy courts and lenders' lawyers alike. One haunted place is the guaranty agreement where complete waivers of all claims against the debtor, developed initially in response to *Deprizio* in an attempt to prevent the guarantor from being a creditor at all, still sometimes terrorize the living.

Bankruptcy Code §§ 547, 550. See also Preference.

## Designation Rights

The right to determine which of the debtor's unexpired leases and executory contracts will be assumed, to whom assumed leases and contracts will be assigned, and the consideration for the assignment of the leases and contracts.

Designation rights are typically sold by the bankruptcy estate to one or more third party bidders. A purchaser of designation rights pays an initial sum to the debtor or trustee, markets the leases or contracts, and then assigns the leases or contracts. After the assignment, the proceeds from the assignment are divided between the estate and the buyer of the designation rights under a court-approved agreement between them.

The debtor usually rejects any leases or contracts that are not assigned within the marketing period.

Designation rights sales are often seen in large commercial retail bankruptcies, such as Montgomery Ward, Kmart, Service Merchandise, and Ames Departments Stores.

There is disagreement among courts and practitioners regarding whether sales of designation rights are authorized by the Code.

Bankruptcy Code § 365. See also Assumption and Assignment of Executory Contracts and Unexpired Leases, Rejection of Executory Contracts and Unexpired Leases.

**DIP**

Acronym for debtor in possession. Pronounced by stating its initials—"D-I-P."

**DIP Financing**

A loan to a debtor in its Chapter 11 case, usually immediately following the filing of the case under "emergency" circumstances.

How the lender controls the case.

Bankruptcy Code § 364. See also Roll-Over.

**Dirt for Debt Plan**

See Eat Dirt Plan.

**Discharge**

An injunction that bars creditors from collecting debts incurred by the debtor before its bankruptcy filing from the debtor or its property after discharge. In a Chapter 11 case, creditors are entitled only to payment of their claims to the extent provided for in a confirmed bankruptcy plan. In a Chapter 7 case, creditors are paid, if at all, by the Chapter 7 trustee from proceeds of the liquidation of the debtor's assets.

Bankruptcy Code §§ 523, 524, 727, 1141(d). See also Co-Debtor, Guarantor.

## Disclosure Statement

A document, similar to a prospectus, that a Chapter 11 plan proponent must file with its Chapter 11 plan. Sometimes as big as a phone book and even less interesting to read.

The purpose of the disclosure statement is to provide information that will enable creditors to make an informed decision whether to accept or reject the plan. A disclosure statement usually includes a history of the debtor leading up to the bankruptcy filing, its current financial and legal state of affairs, and a summary of the proposed Chapter 11 plan.

Solicitation of votes to accept or reject the plan may be made only after distribution of an approved disclosure statement. Creditors may file objections to the proposed disclosure statement. Lenders often use the objection process and the hearing on approval of the disclosure statement to try to convince the court that the plan is hopelessly unconfirmable and that the court should end the case then and there—a tactic that seldom succeeds but does so often enough that lender's counsel feel compelled to keep at it.

Bankruptcy Code § 1125. See also Adequate Information, Solicitation.

## Disgorgement

The word that strikes knee-knocking terror in the minds and hearts of bankruptcy professionals. An order by the bankruptcy court that professionals retained in the case must "disgorge" fees they have been paid on an interim basis prior to final court approval. This is often seen in the context of a case becoming "administratively insolvent"—where there are insufficient assets to pay all administrative expense claims. It may also occur in situations where professionals are found to have (1) violated disinterestedness standards, (2) failed to keep detailed and adequate time records, or (3) been paid an excessive interim amount in light of ultimate results in the case.

See also Professionals' Fees.

## Disguised Financing

A loan masquerading as a sale or lease transaction. A debtor or other estate representative may seek to persuade a bankruptcy court that a lease is actually a loan in order to deprive a lender of the more exalted status of a lessor or buyer (versus a lender) under the Code.

See its antonyms: True Lease, True Sale.

## Disinterestedness

A professional person employed by a debtor, a trustee, or a committee must be "disinterested"—i.e., a person who (1) is not a creditor, an equity holder, or an insider, (2) is not and was not, within two years before the date of the filing of the petition, a director, officer, or employee of the debtor, and (3) does not have an interest materially adverse to the interest of the estate or of any class of creditors or equity security holders by reason of any direct or indirect relationship to, connection with, or interest in, the debtor, or for any other reason.

Bankruptcy Code §§ 101(14), 327(a). See also Disgorgement, Professional Person.

**Dismissal**

The bankruptcy court's decision to dismiss a bankruptcy case, usually in response to a request by the lender or another creditor. Upon dismissal, the debtor and its property no longer have the protections of the Code, including the automatic stay, and creditors are free to resume their pre-bankruptcy efforts to collect their debts.

Be careful what you ask for. Dismissal of the debtor's bankruptcy case also means that creditors lose the benefit of having the debtor and its property subject to the control and watchful eye of the bankruptcy court. Often lenders would rather strike a deal with a creditors' committee or a trustee to use the bankruptcy court to collect and liquidate its collateral in the bankruptcy court because it is often a more convenient forum than state courts or other federal courts.

Bankruptcy Code § 1112.

**Disputed Claim**

Claim asserted against the bankruptcy estate that is in dispute, either because it has been listed as disputed in the debtor's schedules or because the claim has been objected to. The holders of disputed claims are not entitled to vote on a bankruptcy plan unless the claim is temporarily allowed by the bankruptcy court for voting purposes. Until a disputed claim is "allowed" by the court, the holder of the claim is not entitled to any distribution under the plan.

See also Allowed Claim.

**Doctrine of Necessity**

The notion that certain clear language in the Code can be ignored if the situation is of a sufficiently emergent or critical nature. Used to justify various "first day" items including payment of prepetition claims of employees and "critical vendors."

See also Critical Vendor, First Day Motions, First Day Orders.

**Due Process**

A fundamental right of a citizen, protected by the Fifth and Fourteenth Amendments to the United States Constitution, to be free of the taking of its property without due process of law—a constitutional right, some contend, that is routinely denied to creditors in bankruptcy cases. See, for example, Mootness Doctrine.

***Durrett* Case**

Fifth Circuit decision issued in 1980 in which the court ruled that a purchaser at a real estate fore-closure sale conducted under Texas law was liable for a fraudulent transfer.

The purchaser, who was a third party bidder and not the secured lender, was found to be in receipt of a fraudulent transfer when it bid $115,400 at the sale and received title to property that the court later determined had a fair market value of $200,000. In so holding, the court stated that it could find no prior fraudulent transfer decisions that upheld a sale of real property for less than 70 percent of fair market value, prompting many lenders and lawyers to adopt the percentage as a benchmark in devising fore-closure bidding strategies.

*Durrett* met its demise in the U.S. Supreme Court's *BFP* decision, where the court held that the price received at a regularly conducted, noncollusive fore-closure sale conclusively establishes reasonably equivalent value.

See also *BFP* Case, Constructively Fraudulent Transfer, Regularly Conducted Foreclosure Sale.

## Earmarked Loan

A creditor's defense to a preference action that the funds it received as an alleged preference were never property of the debtor because they were not under the debtor's control and were instead "earmarked" for the payment of that creditor and only that creditor. Thus the debtor's property was not diminished by the transaction since it merely substituted one creditor for another. The transferee will not be protected if the estate was diminished by the transaction, such as where the earmarked loan is secured.

Bankruptcy Code § 547. See also Preference.

## Eat Dirt Plan

A Chapter 11 plan under which a debtor or other plan proponent proposes to transfer some of the lender's collateral to the lender as payment in full of the lender's claim, while the debtor keeps the remainder of the lender's collateral free of any claim by the lender.

The credit amount is set by the debtor's plan and approved by the court rather than by the results of an actual sale of the property. This creates the risk that the credit to the lender's claim will be greater than the value the lender can realize from the property. If the lender objects to this treatment, the plan cannot be confirmed unless the bankruptcy court finds that the debtor's "dirt for debt" proposal furnishes the lender the "indubitable equivalent" of its claim—a finding that many courts are reluctant to make because of the inherent difficulties in estimating the value of the lender's collateral.

Bankruptcy Code § 1129(b)(2)(A)(iii). See also Indubitable Equivalent, Reverse Alchemy, Valuation.

## Effective Date

The date that the debtor is to begin performing its obligations under a confirmed Chapter 11 plan. The effective date of a plan is designated in the plan itself and is often a date approximately 10 days after the date that the bankruptcy court confirms the plan.

## Election of Trustee

The right of creditors to elect a trustee to replace the trustee appointed by the United States Trustee or by the court in a Chapter 7 case, or appointed by the court in a Chapter 11 case.

Only those noninsider creditors that hold undisputed, fixed, liquidated, unsecured claims and that do not hold interests materially adverse to other creditors are entitled to vote. Where an election is held in a Chapter 7 case, it is held at the 341 meeting. If creditors do not elect a trustee in a Chapter 7 case, then the interim trustee remains as trustee in the case.

In a Chapter 11 case, if a party in interest wants the opportunity to elect a trustee to replace the trustee appointed by the bankruptcy court, then it must request an election within 30 days after the court makes its appointment.

Bankruptcy Code §§ 702, 1104(b). See also 341 Meeting, Chapter 7 Trustee, Chapter 11 Trustee.

## Entry of Appearance/Request for Notices

A document filed with the bankruptcy clerk to request receipt of notices and pleadings filed in the case.

## Equitable Mootness

See Mootness Doctrine.

## Equitable Subordination

Doctrine that allows the bankruptcy court to subordinate the claim of one creditor to the claim of another for purposes of distribution from the bankruptcy estate if the creditor is guilty of inequitable conduct directly resulting in financial harm to another creditor. A secured creditor whose claim is equitably subordinated may also be required to transfer its lien to the bankruptcy estate.

Bankruptcy Code § 510(c).

## Equities of the Case

Although the lender's security interest in after-acquired property is cut off as of the commencement of the bankruptcy case (see After-Acquired Property Clause), its security interest extends to proceeds, products, offspring, profits, and rents (including hotel revenues) unless the bankruptcy court refuses to allow such extension "based on the equities of the case." Although equities of the case is an obviously

67

vague standard that allows the court a great deal of discretion, it is usually interpreted to require only that the lender pay for the expenses incurred by the debtor in completing or enhancing the collateral in some way, for example where the debtor turns raw materials into finished goods inventory and incurs payroll and other expenses to do so. The lender is not allowed to obtain a windfall by collecting the proceeds without paying the cost of creating the proceeds.

Bankruptcy Code § 552. See also After-Acquired Property Clause.

## Equity Cushion

The value of the lender's collateral in excess of the amount of its claim.

The lender is "oversecured" to the extent of its equity cushion, a generally enviable position in bankruptcy until the debtor uses the lender's oversecured status as an excuse to merely accrue and not pay the over-secured creditor accruing interest and attorneys' fees on its claim while the case is pending. Many argue that it is unnecessary and even illegal to make any payment to the lender after commencement of the case and that, instead, interest and fees should accrue until the equity cushion is exhausted. Others argue that the equity cushion must be maintained, at least at some level. The debtor will also argue, in connection with its motion to use cash collateral, that the equity cushion itself provides sufficient adequate protection to justify the debtor's use of cash collateral even if there is erosion of the cushion.

EXPLODING GUARANTY

NEVER QUESTION THE LENDER'S RIGHTS, DUDE!

*Synonym: Mirage.*

See also Adequate Protection, Cash Collateral, Oversecured Creditor, Use of Cash Collateral.

## Equity Security Holder

The owner of an interest in a business entity such as a corporation, limited liability company or limited partnership. Equity security holders are at the bottom of the bankruptcy food chain.

Bankruptcy Code §§ 101(15), 101(16).

## Equity Security Holders' Committee

A committee in a Chapter 11 case whose purpose is to represent the interests of the debtor's equity interest holders. Members of the committee are chosen by the United States Trustee from the ranks of those who hold equity interests in the debtor. Formerly the Sasquatch of a bankruptcy proceeding, since 2000 this beast has been more frequently sighted.

Bankruptcy Code §§ 1102, 1103. See also Committee.

## Estate

See Bankruptcy Estate.

## Estate Representative

The debtor, the trustee, a committee, an examiner, a trustee of a litigation trust, or other person or entity designated to perform one or more functions on behalf of the bankruptcy estate.

Bankruptcy Code § 1123(b)(4).

## Estimation of Claims

Preliminary determination (but often with very final consequences) of the amount of an unliquidated or contingent claim when a final determination would unduly delay the administration of the bankruptcy case. Estimation can be for either vote counting or distribution purposes, and there may be no spoils left to divide if the final determination is more than the estimate.

Bankruptcy Code § 502(c). See also Allowed Claim.

## Examiner

An independent person appointed by the bankruptcy court to conduct an investigation of the debtor, including any allegations of fraud, dishonesty, incompetence, misconduct, mismanagement, or irregularity in the management of the affairs of the debtor of or by current or former management. The Code requires the appointment of an examiner if requested by a party in interest and the debtor has fixed, liquidated, unsecured debt (other than debt for goods, services, or taxes, or debt owing to an insider) exceeding $5 million.

Bankruptcy Code §§ 1104, 1106.

## Exclusivity Period

That period during which only the debtor may file a Chapter 11 plan. Initially 120 days from the date of the bankruptcy filing, it may be extended by bankruptcy court order up to 18 months from the date of the bankruptcy filing. When the exclusivity period expires, any party in interest may file a plan.

Bankruptcy Code § 1121. See also Competing Plan.

## Executory Contract

Although not all courts agree on what makes a contract "executory," it is generally accepted that a contract is executory if there are continuing or unperformed obligations under the contract by both parties, the breach of which would constitute a material default. A non-executory contract, by contrast, is generally held to be a contract under which one or both of the parties have no remaining duties. An executory contract may be assumed or rejected by the debtor. A non-executory contract is not subject to assumption or rejection.

Bankruptcy Code § 365. See also Assumption and Assignment of Executory Contracts and Unexpired Leases, Rejection of Executory Contracts and Unexpired Leases.

## Exploding Guaranty

A term sometimes used to describe a guaranty imposing personal liability for an otherwise nonre-course debt if the borrower contests the lender's rights in a bankruptcy case. The more commonly used term is Springing Guaranty.

See also Springing Guaranty.

## Fair and Equitable Test

One of the requirements for confirmation of a Chapter 11 plan over the objection of an impaired, non-accepting class of creditors.

To pass the fair and equitable test regarding a class of *secured* claims, the plan must provide, among other things, that (1) each holder of a claim in that class retain its lien and (2) each holder of a claim in that class be paid the present value of its secured claim or, if the lender's collateral is to be sold, that the lender's lien attach to the sale proceeds.

The plan may also meet the fair and equitable test with respect to a class of secured claims by providing each of the creditors in the class with the "indubitable equivalent" of its claim (see Indubitable Equivalent).

To satisfy the fair and equitable test regarding a class of *unsecured* claims, a plan must not violate the absolute priority rule (see Absolute Priority Rule).

Bankruptcy Code § 1129(b)(2). See also Absolute Priority Rule, Confirmation Requirements, Cramdown, Cramdown Interest Rate, Indubitable Equivalent.

## Feasibility Test

The ability of the debtor to meet its plan obligations post-confirmation. As a condition to confirmation, a plan proponent must show that the plan is "feasible"—that it is not likely to be followed by the need for liquidation or further financial reorganization of the debtor (other than a liquidation proposed in the plan itself).

Bankruptcy Code § 1129(a)(11). See also Confirmation Requirements.

## Federal Rules of Bankruptcy Procedure

Written rules of procedure governing practice before the bankruptcy court.

## Fee Application

A pleading filed by a professional person retained by the trustee, debtor, or an officially appointed com-mittee requesting bankruptcy court approval of payment of the fees and costs incurred by that professional in connection with its employment in the bankruptcy case. Fee applications are subject to review and objection by all parties in interest in a Chapter 11 case.

See also Professional Person.

**Final Order**

A court order as to which the time to appeal, petition for *certiorari*, or move for reargument or rehearing has expired and as to which no appeal, petition for *certiorari*, or other proceedings for reargument or rehearing is pending.

Parties affected by a bankruptcy court order typically wait until the order becomes a final order before acting on the order out of concern that the order might be reversed, vacated, or modified by an appellate court or by the bankruptcy court itself. Sometimes, however, the parties proceed even though an order has not become final, in the hope of successfully invoking the Mootness Doctrine.

See also Mootness Doctrine.

**Finality**

See Final Order.

**Financial Contracts**

See Financial Markets Contracts.

## Financial Markets Contracts

Repurchase agreements, swap agreements, commodity contracts, forward contracts, and securities contracts (defined in Section 741) that are treated more favorably than most other executory contracts under the Code on the theory that the financial markets would be unduly disrupted absent such favorable treatment. For example, certain types of setoff under such contracts may be accomplished without seeking relief from the automatic stay.

Bankruptcy Code §§ 101(25), 101(47), 101(53B), 362(b)(6), 362(b)(7), 362(b)(17), 741(7). See also Automatic Stay, Executory Contract, Setoff.

## First Day Motions

Pleadings usually filed along with the Chapter 11 petition seeking emergency relief, with minimal notice and opportunity for a hearing, so that a debtor may conduct its business and administer its bankruptcy postpetition without interruption. Common first-day motions include motions to address the following issues: joint administration of related bankruptcy cases; notice and administrative procedures; obtaining employment of attorneys and other professionals; procedures for payment of interim professional fees and expenses; extension of time to file schedules and statement of financial affairs; approving cash management systems; payment of the prepetition claims of critical vendors and employees, continuation of customer programs, providing adequate assurance for utilities; establishing reclamation procedures; and authorization for use of cash collateral or debtor-in-possession financing.

See also Doctrine of Necessity, Due Process.

## First Day Orders

Orders granting first day motions filed by the debtor, often entered by the bankruptcy court with little or no notice to creditors.

See Doctrine of Necessity, Due Process, First Day Motions.

## First Meeting of Creditors

See 341 Meeting.

## Forced Loan Approach

See Coerced Loan Approach.

## Formula Approach

One of the methods that bankruptcy courts use to set the cramdown interest rate that a bankruptcy plan must provide to a secured creditor that does not accept the plan. Under the formula approach the court starts with a base rate and then adjusts that rate upward by assessing the risk associated with the facts of the case.

The rates that courts have primarily used to determine the base rate are the prime rate (referred to as the "prime plus formula approach") and the rate on a United States Treasury instrument (referred to as the "treasury rate formula approach").

The risk premium is determined by reference to such factors as the debtor's credit history, the nature of the collateral, the length of repayment, and the viability of the reorganization plan.

See also Coerced Loan Approach, Cost of Funds Approach, Cramdown, Cramdown Interest Rate,

Forced Loan Approach, Market Rate Approach, Presumptive Contract Rate Approach, Prime Plus Formula Approach, Treasury Plus Formula Approach.

## Fraudulent Conveyance

See Fraudulent Transfer.

## Fraudulent Transfer

A transfer by the debtor (including the incurring of an obligation by the debtor) voidable under Section 548 or under state law imported into the bankruptcy case through Section 544.

A party attacking a transfer under Section 548 must show that the transfer occurred on or within two years of the date of the debtor's bankruptcy filing. In addition, it must be shown that the debtor either (1) made the transfer with the actual intent to hinder, delay or defraud any entity to which the debtor was or became, on or after the date of the transfer, indebted, or (2) received less than reasonably equivalent value in exchange for the transfer.

Finally, the party seeking to avoid the transfer must show that (a) the debtor was insolvent on the date of the transfer or became insolvent because of the transfer, (b) the debtor was engaged in business or a transaction, or was about to engage in business or a transaction, for which any property remaining with the debtor was an unreasonably small capital, (c) the debtor intended to incur, or believed that the debtor would incur, debts that would be beyond the debtor's ability to pay as such debts matured, or (d) the debtor made the transfer to or for the benefit of an insider under an employment contract and not in the ordinary course of business.

Forty-three states and the District of Columbia have

enacted the Uniform Fraudulent Transfer Act ("UFTA"), similar to Section 548 in purpose and application. In Maryland and New York, transfers by the debtor may be attacked under the Uniform Fraudulent Conveyance Act ("UFCA"), also similar to Section 548. The remaining states (Alaska, Kentucky, Louisiana, South Carolina, and Virginia) have state-specific fraudulent transfer statutes. The look-back period for actions under UFTA and UFCA is generally four years (as contrasted with the two-year look-back period under Section 548). Estate representatives are sometimes able to take advantage of this longer look-back period by employing the strong arm powers of Section 544.

Bankruptcy Code §§ 544, 548, 550. See also Avoidance Action, *BFP* Case, Constructively Fraudulent Transfer, *Durrett* Case, Intentionally Fraudulent Transfer, Regularly Conducted Foreclosure Sale, Strong Arm Powers, Transfer.

## General Unsecured Claim

A claim for which a creditor holds no collateral (or whose lien on the collateral is avoided under one of the avoidance sections of the Code) or does not enjoy any statutory priority (statutory priority claims include certain wage and tax claims and, post-BAPCA, certain claims for goods delivered shortly before the bankruptcy filing).

If there are funds available to pay general unsecured claims, these claims are paid in proportion to the amount of the claim relative to the total of all allowed general unsecured claims.

General unsecured status is, for the most part, a fate only slightly better than death, sometimes worse in that the creditor may incur expenses in the bankruptcy case for little or no return, thus "throwing good money after bad."

See also Administrative Claim, Priority Claim, Reclamation Claim, Secured Claim.

## General Unsecured Creditor

A creditor who holds a general unsecured claim.

## Gerrymandering

Improperly classifying claims under a Chapter 11 plan in order to manufacture an impaired, accepting class of creditors to meet the One-Impaired-Class-Must-Accept-The-Plan Rule. For example, a debtor may attempt to classify the lender's unsecured deficiency claim separately from the claims of other unsecured creditors if the lender's deficiency claim is large enough that a "no" vote from the lender will cause the unsecured class to reject the plan, leaving the debtor with no impaired accepting class and therefore unable to obtain confirmation of its plan. A debtor or other plan proponent may also try to separately classify claims of friendly unsecured creditors into a separate accepting class.

Bankruptcy Code §§ 1122, 1124, 1129. See also Classification of Claims, Cramdown, One-Impaired-Class-Must-Accept-The-Plan Rule.

## Going Concern Value

The value of a business assuming it will continue in operation, thus likely including an effective mark-up of the asset value based on the continuing "goodwill" and ability of the business to generate income. Whether a debtor's business is valued on a going concern or on a liquidation basis can be the critical factor in determining whether a creditor is over-secured or undersecured, whether and to what extent it is entitled to adequate protection, and whether a plan is fair and equitable and otherwise satisfies plan confirmation requirements.

See also Adequate Protection, Confirmation Requirements, Liquidation Value, Oversecured Creditor, Undersecured Creditor, Valuation.

## Good Faith

Honesty of intention, freedom from knowledge of circumstances that would put a reasonable person on inquiry, and an absence of design to gain an improper advantage. Referred to by courts as an "overriding principle of bankruptcy administration," the concept comes into play throughout a bankruptcy case—from the filing of the case, to the protection of certain persons doing business with the estate, to the potential applicability of certain defenses asserted by a transferee, to the filing of a plan. For example:

- If a debtor files a bankruptcy case with a lack of good faith, cause exists for the bankruptcy court to dismiss the bankruptcy.

- The validity of a transaction by which a third party has acquired property of the estate will not be affected by a reversal or modification on appeal of the order that authorized the sale, if the third party acted with good faith (and if the transaction was not stayed pending appeal).

- The validity of a lending transaction, and the validity of a lien taken in connection with such lending, will not be affected by a reversal or modification on appeal of the order that authorized the loan, if the party lending money to the estate acted with good faith (and if the lending transaction was not stayed pending appeal).

- A transferee liable for a fraudulent transfer is entitled to a lien on the property it is required to return to the estate, but only to the extent of the value it gave to the debtor at the time of the transfer and only if it received the transfer in good faith.

- A subsequent transferee of an avoidable transfer (i.e., someone other than the initial transferee who took directly from the debtor) is not liable for the avoidable transfer if it took for value, in good faith, and without knowledge of the voidability of the transfer.

A Chapter 11 plan can be confirmed by a bankruptcy court only if certain requirements are met, one being that the plan be filed in good faith and not by any means forbidden by law.

Bankruptcy Code §§ 363(m), 364(e), 550(b), 550(d), 1112(b)(1), 1129(a)(3). See also, Bad Faith Filing, Dismissal, Immediate Transferee, Mediate Transferee, Subsequent Transferee.

## Ground Lease

A lease of land (often before any building has been erected on the land), usually for a very long term. Any improvements usually revert to the ground lease landlord on termination of the lease.

Lenders often lend to ground lease tenants on the security of their leasehold interests. Complications ensue if the tenant files bankruptcy and rejects the lease, thus exposing the lender to loss of its collateral unless it has a Subordination, Nondisturbance and Attornment Agreement ("SNDA") with, or some other enforceable assurance from, the ground lease landlord enabling the lender or its designee to continue in possession notwithstanding the rejection. Further complications may ensue if the ground lease *landlord* files bankruptcy and attempts to reject its obligations under the SNDA.

See also Rejection, Subordination, Nondisturbance and Attornment Agreement.

## Guarantor

One who agrees to be liable for the debt of another, sometimes described as a "fool with a pen."

A guarantor who pays a debt validly owed by a debtor in bankruptcy is in most instances subrogated to the rights that the creditor has against the debtor to the extent of such payment unless the guarantor has some other right of reimbursement.

The Code makes it clear that the discharge of a debtor in a Chapter 7 or Chapter 11 case does not have the effect of discharging the obligations of a guarantor, yet plan proponents frequently seek discharges (or the equivalent thereof in the form of permanent injunctions) in favor of guarantors in their plans.

Bankruptcy Code §§ 509, 524(e). See also Co-Debtor, Co-Obligor, Subrogation Rights.

## Hotel Revenues

Revenues from the operation of a hotel or other lodging property. Although they are sometimes characterized as "rents," they are usually determined to be "accounts" or "general intangibles" (primarily because they arise as much from the provision of services as from the temporary occupancy of hotel rooms).

For a time, only "rents" were entitled to protection as proceeds under Sections 363(a) and 552, and some courts ruled that hotel revenues were not "rents" and thus not entitled to that protection. Congress came to the rescue of hotel lenders by amending the Code to protect both rents *per se* and also "the fees, charges, accounts, or other payments for the use or occupancy of rooms and other public facilities in hotels, motels or other lodging properties." But this relief should not confuse the fact that a lender must not rely merely on its Assignment of Leases and Rents to perfect its security interest in hotel revenues, which are most often judicially characterized not as rents but as "accounts" or "general intangibles" under the Uniform Commercial Code. Thus, a purported security interest in rights to payment connected with a hotel operation perfected only through an Assignment of Leases and Rents is likely to be avoided by application of the strong arm powers under Section 544.

Bankruptcy Code §§ 363(a), 552(b)(2). See also Cash Collateral, Nursing Home Revenues, Strong Arm Powers.

## Hypothetical Lien Creditor

One of the strong arm powers given to a debtor is the ability to assume the identity of a hypothetical lien creditor. Wearing the hat of a hypothetical lien creditor, the debtor is able to avoid certain liens or other transfers of interests in the debtor's property. Especially vulnerable are liens or transfers that are not properly recorded. For example, the debtor can assume the guise of a judicial lien creditor (whether or not a judicial lien creditor actually exists) or a creditor who obtains a right of execution against the debtor (whether or not such a creditor actually exists). Any lien or other transfer of property by a debtor that would be avoidable by either of these types of hypothetical lien creditors under non-bankruptcy law is avoidable by the debtor.

Bankruptcy Code § 544(a). See also Avoidance Action, Judicial Lien, Strong Arm Powers.

## Immediate Transferee

The transferee from the initial transferee. The second transferee, and in contrast under the Code to an "initial transferee" (the one who received the transfer directly from the debtor) and a "mediate transferee" (who is third in line or beyond and who received a transfer from the immediate transferee or from a preceding mediate transferee).

The classification is relevant in terms of the defenses available to the transferee of an avoidable transfer. An immediate or mediate transferee, but not an initial transferee, may escape liability if it took the transfer for value, in good faith, and without knowledge of the voidability of the transfer.

Bankruptcy Code § 550(a)(1), (2). See also Avoidable Transfer, Avoidance Action, Initial Transferee, Mediate Transferee, Subsequent Transferee.

## Impairment

Proposed alteration of a creditor's or equity interest holder's legal, equitable, or contractual rights under a Chapter 11 plan. For example, a lender's claim is an impaired claim if the plan modifies the maturity date, interest rate, or *any* provision of the lender's loan documents even if the Chapter 11 plan provides for payment in full of the claim and even if the modification *favors* the lender (such as an increase in the contractual interest rate).

Bankruptcy Code § 1124. See also Artificial Impairment, Impaired Class, Non-Impairment Plan, One-Impaired-Class-Must-Accept-The-Plan Rule.

## Impaired Class

A class of creditors or equity interest holders whose legal, equitable, or contractual rights are altered by a proposed Chapter 11 plan.

Lenders frequently hold a claim for accelerated payment on account of a default by the borrower. A plan may treat such a claim as "unimpaired" despite the acceleration if the plan meets the requirements of Section 1124(2).

Bankruptcy Code § 1124. See also Impairment, One-Impaired-Class-Must-Accept-The-Plan Rule.

## Improvement in Position Test

A calculation that determines whether a lender with a floating lien on inventory or accounts receivable has received a preference. The bankruptcy court compares the value of the lender's collateral as of 90 days prior to the bankruptcy filing with the value of the same collateral on the bankruptcy filing date. If the net result is that the secured creditor's position has not improved from the applicable period to the bankruptcy filing date, there is no preference.

Bankruptcy Code § 547(c)(5). See also Preference.

**Incurable Default**

A default by a debtor that is not subject to cure, thereby potentially preventing assumption of an executory contract or unexpired lease under Section 365. For example, if a tenant violates a use clause pre-bankruptcy, the debtor or trustee cannot travel back in time and change the fact that the property has not been used as required by the lease. Congress attempted to cure this problem in BAPCA, but the cure only extends to the assumption of real estate leases, not to personal property leases and executory contracts.

Bankruptcy Code §§ 365(b)(1)(A), 365(b)(2), 1124(2)(A). See also Assumption and Assignment of Executory Contracts and Unexpired Leases, Rejection of Executory Contracts and Unexpired Leases.

**Independent Director**

Conceived in credit rating agency laboratories in New York, this creature supposedly guards the doors of the bankruptcy courts from feckless debtors bearing frivolous bankruptcy petitions.

According to the standard rating agency definition, a member of the board of directors or managers of a corporation or limited liability company who has not been, while serving as a director or manager of the entity or within the preceding five years, any of the following: (1) a direct or indirect legal or beneficial owner of the entity or any of its affiliates; (2) a creditor, supplier, customer, employee, officer, director, family member, manager, or contractor of the entity or any of its affiliates; or (3) a person who directly or indirectly controls the entity or any of its affiliates, or any creditor supplier, employee, officer, director, manager or contractor of the entity or any of its affiliates.

See also Bankruptcy Proof, Securitization, Special (or Single) Purpose Bankruptcy Remote Entity.

## Indirect Preference

A preference resulting from a transfer by the debtor to one entity that results in a benefit to a second entity, thus rendering the second entity liable for a preference. An indirect preference occurs, for example, where a debtor pays a debt that is guaranteed; the payment, although not to the guarantor, reduces the guarantor's exposure and thus is "for the benefit of" the guarantor.

Bankruptcy Code §§ 547(b)(1), 550(a)(1). See also *Deprizio* Doctrine, Preference.

## Indubitable Equivalent

Something that is supposedly undoubtedly equal in value to what is taken away.

A "catch all" form of adequate protection under the Code requiring that a debtor provide a creditor with something having a value that is the "indubitable equivalent" of the amount of diminution in value of the creditor's collateral resulting from its use in the bankruptcy case.

It is also one means of providing "fair and equitable" treatment to a secured creditor under a Chapter 11 plan, i.e., by providing the creditor with the "indubitable equivalent" of its claim. In a typical Chapter 11 plan involving the claim of a lender the debtor most often attempts to satisfy the lender's right to "fair and equitable treatment" by providing the lender with periodic payments sufficient to pay the secured claim in full, with interest, while the lender retains its lien under the plan. A second option for the debtor to satisfy the fair and equitable test is for the plan to provide for a sale of the lender's collateral, free and clear of the lender's lien, with the lien to attach to the sale proceeds. The third option—providing the lender with the "indubitable equivalent" of its claim—is less well defined than the first two options.

The courts have only outlined the contours of the term in decisions accepting and rejecting various plan treatments offered by proponents as providing a lender the indubitable equivalent of its secured claim. For example:

- A lender does not receive the indubitable equivalent of its claim if the debtor substitutes a letter of credit for the lender's collateral, but the letter of credit is subject to ambiguities in the letter of credit accommodations.

- There is no indubitable equivalence where a debtor substitutes equity securities for the lender's collateral if the value of the securities is questionable.

- If the debtor is to transfer property to the lender as the indubitable equivalent of the lender's secured claim, the property must produce cash flow or be capable of being sold within a reasonable time so that the lender can realize cash.

Bankruptcy Code §§ 361(3), 1129(b)(2)(A)(iii). See also Adequate Protection, Confirmation Requirements, Cramdown, Eat Dirt Plan, Fair and Equitable Test, Reverse Alchemy.

## Initial Transferee

The first transferee of an avoidable transfer, i.e., the party that received the transfer directly from the debtor. The Code provides that a trustee or debtor in possession may recover property, or the value of the property, preferentially or fraudulently transferred to the initial transferee or the entity for whose benefit (e.g., a lender or guarantor) such transfer was made even though the initial transferee received the transfer in good faith and without knowledge of its voidability.

Bankruptcy Code § 550(a)(1), (2). See also Avoidance Action, Fraudulent Transfer, Immediate Transferee, Mediate Transferee, Preference.

## Insider

A person or entity having a close enough relationship with or connection to the debtor to require special scrutiny of its dealings with the debtor. Relatives of individual debtors, officers and directors of corporate debtors, general partners of partnership debtors, "managing agents," and "persons in control" of debtors fall within the definition of "insider." An "affiliate" of the debtor or an insider of such affiliate is also defined as an "insider."

Insiders have potential liability for avoidance of preferences made within one year prior to the bankruptcy filing; by contrast, the look-back period for non-insiders is only 90 days.

Bankruptcy Code §§ 101(2), 101(31). See also Affiliate, Indirect Preference, Preference.

**Insolvent**

An ugly word to the business owner and to its secured lender. A less ugly word to the bankruptcy practitioner, at least until the word "administratively" is attached to it.

Defined by the Code as a financial condition such that an entity's debts are greater than the fair value of the entity's property, not including exempt property and not including property transferred, concealed, or removed with an intent to hinder, delay or defraud the entity's creditors. In determining whether a general partnership is insolvent, the aggregate value of the non-partnership property of each general partner in excess of the amount of the non-partnership debt owed by each general partner is added to the value of the general partnership's property.

Bankruptcy Code § 101(32). See also Administratively Insolvent, Fraudulent Transfer, Preference.

**Intentionally Fraudulent Transfer**

A transfer by the debtor of its property made with actual intent to hinder, delay, or defraud creditors. Fraudulent transfers occurring within two years prior to the bankruptcy filing are avoidable under Section 548 in bankruptcy cases filed on or after October 17, 2006 (or within one year in bankruptcy cases filed before October 17, 2006). State fraudulent transfer statutes are imported into the Code through Section 544. Those statutes usually have a longer look-back period (four years is common).

Bankruptcy Code § 548(a)(1)(A). See also Avoidance Action, Constructively Fraudulent Transfer, Fraudulent Transfer.

## Intercreditor Agreement

An agreement between creditors, usually secured creditors, with respect to various matters including lien priority, standstill provisions, and waivers by the junior creditor including waivers of various rights in a future bankruptcy case of the borrower—for example, waivers of the right to file or join in an involuntary petition, the right to vote in favor of a plan not approved by the senior creditor, the right to adequate protection, and the right to object to various measures supported by the senior creditor including DIP financing and adequate protection proposals favoring the senior creditor.

The intercreditor agreement has furnished the bedrock upon which the lenders and borrowers in CMBS lending have erected a massive and extraordinarily complex structure of billions of dollars of senior and mezzanine debt. The enforceability of the bankruptcy waivers in the industry-standard agreement are frequently questioned and have not been tested due to the low-default environment of the last 15 years (1992-2007).

Section 510(c) requires enforcement of "subordination agreements," but that could be interpreted narrowly to enforce only the lien priority provisions of the agreement. If the bankruptcy courts were to invalidate the waiver provisions of the agreement, especially the waiver of the right to propose, vote for, or otherwise support a plan unfriendly to the senior lender, the single asset real estate field could become a lively and thriving metropolis rather than the ghost town it is in the middle of the first decade of the 21$^{st}$ century.

Bankruptcy Code § 510(c). See also A-B Note Structure, Mezzanine Debt, Securitization, Subordination.

## Interest

1. Payment for the use of someone else's money. What you do not get in bankruptcy if you are undersecured. What you get to accrue but not necessarily receive current payment of if you are oversecured. But see Single Asset Real Estate.

2. Something (a lien, ownership interest, tenancy or other unspecified "interest") that property can be sold free and clear of under Section 363(f). This interest will attach to the sale "proceeds" of which there may or may not be enough to fully compensate the holder of the interest for its loss.

3. An ownership interest in an entity. Last and least in the bankruptcy process except to the extent that the ownership controls management of the debtor in possession.

Bankruptcy Code §§ 363(f), 506. See also Equity Security Holder, Equity Security Holders' Committee, Oversecured Creditor, Single Asset Real Estate, Undersecured Creditor.

## Interest Rate Swap

An agreement by which a party agrees to make payments to another party on a notional principal amount at a fixed or floating rate in exchange for the counterparty's agreement to make payments based on the inverse rate basis (fixed for floating, floating for fixed). Lenders will often require a debtor that has agreed to pay a floating rate to purchase a swap from a counterparty that will effectively provide the certainty of a fixed rate of interest on the debt. These have proliferated in a low-default environment and so are untested in bankruptcy but may raise interesting issues regarding, among other things, enforceability and whether they can be modified by a plan (especially when the counterparty is the lender).

Bankruptcy Code § 560.

## Involuntary Bankruptcy Petition

A bankruptcy petition filed by a debtor's creditors against the debtor, forcing the debtor into bankruptcy on an involuntary basis.

Bankruptcy Code § 303. See also Involuntary Case, Voluntary Bankruptcy Petition.

## Involuntary Bankruptcy Case

A bankruptcy case of a debtor initiated by *creditors* (or, in the case of a general partnership, by a general partner) through the filing of an involuntary bankruptcy petition against the debtor.

If the debtor has 12 or more creditors, an involuntary case can only be filed if (1) three or more creditors are willing to join in the filing, (2) their claims are not contingent as to liability or subject to a bona fide dispute as to liability or amount, and (3) the total of their claims is at least $12,300 (by statute, this figure is subject to periodic increases) more than the value of any collateral they hold. If the debtor has less than 12 creditors, an involuntary case can be filed by a single creditor whose claim or claims otherwise meets these same requirements.

If a court dismisses an involuntary petition because it contains a materially false statement, it can impose costs and attorneys' fees on the petitioners and can impose actual and punitive damages on a petitioner that "filed the petition in bad faith."

Bankruptcy Code § 303. See also Involuntary Bankruptcy Petition.

## *Ipso Facto* Clause/Provision

A contract clause that terminates or modifies, or grants the non-debtor party the right to terminate or modify, the contract upon the debtor's bankruptcy filing or the insolvency or financial condition of the debtor. The Code does not use the phrase "*ipso facto* clause" but refers, instead, more verbosely (but also more precisely) to "a provision in such contract or lease that is conditioned on—(A) the insolvency or financial condition of the debtor at any time before the closing of the case, (B) the commencement of a case under this title, or (C) the appointment of or taking possession by a trustee in a case under this title or a custodian before such commencement . . ."

Most *ipso facto* clauses in most circumstances are unenforceable, leading to the common misconception that the Code voids all *ipso facto* clauses for all purposes. The Code only voids *ipso facto* clauses for certain purposes and only under certain circumstances.

For example, under Section 541(c)(1)(B), an interest of the debtor becomes property of the estate despite any *ipso facto* clause. Under Section 363(1), the debtor may use, sell, or lease property despite an *ipso facto* clause. Subject to meeting the requirements of Section 365, the debtor may also assign an executory contract or unexpired lease despite an *ipso facto* clause purporting to bar assignment upon the debtor's bankruptcy filing (see Assumption and Assignment of Executory Contracts and Unexpired Leases).

Under Section 365(e), a contract may not be terminated or modified due to an *ipso facto* clause unless the contract is a "personal service contract," that is, a contract where "applicable law excuses a party, other than the debtor, to such contract or lease from accepting performance from or rendering performance to the trustee or to an assignee of such contract or lease, whether or not such contract or lease prohibits or restricts assignment of rights or delegation of duties." (See Personal Service Contract). Thus, the Code actually reads into a "personal service contract" an *ipso facto* clause even if the contract itself does not contain one. Likewise, while Section 365(f) generally voids *ipso facto* clauses terminating or modifying a contract on assumption or assignment by the trustee or debtor, "personal service contracts" are again exempted by Section 365(c) whether or not they contain a provision restricting or preventing assignment or delegation of duties.

Bankruptcy Code §§ 363(1), 365(c), 365(e), 365(f), 541(c)(1)(B). See also Assumption and Assignment of Executory Contracts and Unexpired Leases, Executory Contract, Personal Service Contract.

## Joint Case

A bankruptcy case filed by an individual debtor and the debtor's spouse under a single petition.

Bankruptcy Code § 302. See also Administrative Consolidation, Jointly Administered, Substantive Consolidation.

## Jointly Administered

See Administrative Consolidation.

## Judicial Lien

Lien obtained by judgment, levy, sequestration, or other legal or equitable process or proceeding.

Bankruptcy Code § 101(36). See also Hypothetical Lien Creditor, Strong Arm Powers.

## Landlord Claim

The claim against the bankruptcy estate held by the lessor of real property. The claim may have a number of components:

First, a landlord may have under Section 502(b)(6)(B) a general unsecured claim for any prepetition rent and other charges due under the lease as of the bankruptcy filing. This claim for prepetition unpaid rent, unlike a claim for future rent, is not subject to a monetary cap (see below)).

Second, a landlord may also have an administrative expense claim for any postpetition unpaid rent and other charges due under the lease for the period the tenant uses the property prior to rejection of the lease.

Third, a landlord may also have a general unsecured claim for damages for future rent resulting from a rejection by the debtor of its lease. Such lease rejection damages are capped by Section 502(b)(6)(A). This Code provision limits a landlord's claim to the rent reserved under the lease for the greater of one year or 15 percent of the remaining lease term not to exceed three years.

Finally, a landlord may also have additional rejection damages, such as for repair and maintenance damage claims.

Bankruptcy Code § 502(b)(6). See also Rejection of Executory Contracts and Unexpired Leases.

## *LaSalle*

French adventurer best known for the exploration of Canada and also the name of a Supreme Court decision that addressed the idea of requiring an auction or other competition for the equity in a

Chapter 11 debtor, each opening a vast and uncertain wilderness to be tamed by later generations.

The Supreme Court decision ruled that a Chapter 11 plan violates the absolute priority rule, and thus cannot be confirmed, if the debtor's equity holders are allowed to retain their equity interests in the debtor "without extending an opportunity to anyone else either to compete for that equity or to propose a competing reorganization plan."

Bankruptcy Code § 1129(b)(2)(B)(ii). See also Absolute Priority Rule, *LaSalle* Auction Plan.

### *LaSalle* Auction Plan

A Chapter 11 plan where the debtor's existing equity holders are permitted to acquire post-confirmation ownership of the reorganized debtor by purchasing the equity at an open auction at which creditors and others may bid.

The absolute priority rule prohibits equity holders from retaining their equity interests in the debtor "on account of" those interests if a class of unsecured creditors whose claims are impaired under the plan do not accept the plan. Under a *LaSalle* auction plan, the equity holders argue that they are not receiving equity interests in the reorganized debtor on account of their previous equity in the debtor, but are instead acquiring their interests by virtue of winning the auction.

The *LaSalle* auction plan is so named because the United States Supreme Court in *Bank of America Nation Trust and Savings Association v. 203 N. LaSalle Street Partnership*, mentioned the auction strategy as *possibly* satisfying the absolute priority rule. The court in the *LaSalle* case, while hinting that the auction strategy might work if a plan were otherwise confirmable, did not actually decide whether an auction would satisfy the absolute priority rule because the plan in the *LaSalle* case did not provide for an auction.

*Diabolical questions: May a secured lender credit bid at the auction? Is an open auction enough, or must parties in interest also be allowed to file competing plans? Must such a plan satisfy the old "new value" standards? Or did LaSalle effectively render "new value" plans obsolete?*

Bankruptcy Code § 1129(b)(2)(B)(ii). See also Absolute Priority Rule, Accepting Class, Cramdown, Impaired Class, *LaSalle*, New Value Exception, New Value Plan, Reorganized Debtor.

**Late Charges**

From the debtor's perspective, a charge tacked on by a gluttonous lender who is already charging the debtor for default interest and any fees and costs, including attorneys' fees, incurred by the lender in collecting the debt owed to it and in protecting its collateral. From the secured lender's perspective, a legitimate charge, properly passed on to a debtor or borrower, designed to compensate the lender (1) for the lender's lost use of the money to which it would have had access had the payment been timely made and/or (2) for the lender's increased administrative cost that naturally accrues when one of its loans is paid late.

If there is sufficient collateral value to cover it and the bankruptcy court determines it to be "reasonable," this charge may be added to the lender's secured claim under Section 506(b).

Bankruptcy Code § 506(b). See also Oversecured Creditor, Secured Claim, Undersecured Creditor.

## Leasehold Mortgage

A mortgage not on a fee interest but on the tenant's leasehold interest in property. Vulnerable to rejection of the leasehold by the lender's borrower (the tenant) in the borrower/tenant's bankruptcy.

See also Ground Lease, Rejection of Executory Contracts and Unexpired Leases, Subordination, Nondisturbance, and Attornment Agreement.

## Leveraged Buyout

A transaction by which the existing owners of an entity sell their interests in an entity and are paid from assets of the entity itself or from proceeds of a loan secured by the assets of the entity. This creates a possible fraudulent transfer problem for the buyer's lender because it is receiving collateral from the debtor for loan proceeds that are benefiting the debtor's owners but not the debtor and its creditors.

See also Fraudulent Transfer.

## Lien

A charge against or interest in property to secure payment of a debt or performance of an obligation.

Bankruptcy Code § 101(37).

## Lien Avoidance

The avoidance of a lien or security interest by a trustee or debtor as a preferential or fraudulent transfer or under the strong arm powers under the Code. A misnomer in that the affected lien is not "avoided" but, instead, is transferred to the debtor or trustee for the benefit of the bankruptcy estate.

Thus, the value of the lien is preserved for the estate as a whole rather than simply allowing a junior secured creditor to improve its priority position following avoidance of the lien.

Bankruptcy Code §§ 544, 547, 548, 551. See also Avoidance Action, Fraudulent Transfer, Preference, Strong Arm Powers.

## Liquidating Chapter 11

A Chapter 11 case whose purpose is (or becomes during its course) a liquidation rather than a reorganization of the debtor. A liquidating Chapter 11 is usually preferable to non-bankruptcy liquidation in that it is more orderly and occurs in one forum, preventing a haphazard dismemberment of the debtor due to multiple creditors racing to any number of courthouses, exercising their rights independently and without any coordination with each other or with the debtor.

Bankruptcy Code § 1129(a)(11). See also Liquidating Plan.

*Synonym: "Trustee Avoidance Plan."*

## Liquidating Plan

A plan filed to implement a liquidating Chapter 11.

Bankruptcy Code § 1129(a)(11). See also Liquidating Chapter 11.

## Liquidating Trust

A trust established under a liquidating Chapter 11 plan. Under a typical trust agreement, the trustee is given responsibility for liquidating the debtor's assets, prosecuting avoidance actions, objecting to claims, and disbursing the bankruptcy estate's assets to creditors as provided for under the plan.

See also Liquidating Chapter 11, Liquidating Plan.

## Liquidating Trustee

The trustee under a liquidating trust.

See also Liquidating Chapter 11, Liquidating Plan, Liquidating Trust.

## Liquidation

The process of converting non-cash assets into cash by sale or other disposition. This term is also sometimes used as a synonym for "Chapter 7 case" as the object of Chapter 7 is to liquidate the debtor's assets and distribute the proceeds to creditors. But liquidation is often accomplished in Chapter 11.

See also Liquidating Chapter 11, Liquidating Plan.

## Liquidated Claim

A claim whose dollar amount has been fixed in a precise amount.

**Liquidation Value**

The value of assets assuming they will not be sold as part of a continuing business and thus without a mark-up deriving from their ability to continue to generate income.

See also Going Concern Value, Valuation of Collateral.

**Lock-Up Agreement**

In the bankruptcy context, a contract whereby a party (often the debtor's key lender or block of institutional debt holders) commits itself to support a particular restructuring plan, subject to various terms and conditions. The non-debtor party to a lock-up agreement binds itself to vote for a Chapter 11 plan as long as certain key provisions are included in the plan.

Lock-up agreements are often executed in connection with pre-negotiated Chapter 11 cases, and are usually agreed to and fully executed before the filing of the debtor's Chapter 11 case. A lock-up agreement entered into *post*petition and before distribution of a court-approved disclosure statement usually is but may not be enforced by the court.

See also Adequate Information, Disclosure Statement, Prepackaged Plan.

**Lopucki**

Gadfly law professor who has enraged much of the bankruptcy bar and judiciary by contending that the competition among bankruptcy courts, especially the Delaware and New York courts, to attract large reorganization cases has corrupted the bankruptcy courts and led to unnecessary failures of reorganizing companies.

See also Chapter 22.

**Market Rate Approach**

Any of a number of methods that sets a cramdown interest rate by reference to an interest rate determined in a commercial market (such as the prime rate, the treasury bill rate, or federal funds rate). Many bankruptcy courts have ruled that a secured creditor who does not accept the plan is entitled to interest on its secured claim at a "market rate," but the courts disagree on the precise definition of "market rate" and the methodology for determining the "market rate."

In the most frequent application of the market rate method, courts treat the plan as creating a "forced loan" by the lender and then set the cramdown interest rate at the rate that the lender would receive in the open market for making a loan of similar duration and risk. This version of the market rate approach is referred to as the forced-loan approach or coerced loan approach (see Coerced Loan Approach). Some commentators and practitioners imprecisely use the terms "market rate approach" and "coerced loan approach" as if interchangeable, probably because the coerced-loan approach is the method most often used by courts that subscribe to the idea that the cramdown rate should be linked to a market rate of interest.

See also Coerced Loan Approach, Cost of Funds Approach, Cramdown, Cramdown Interest Rate, Forced Loan Approach, Formula Approach, Presumptive Contract Rate Approach, Prime Plus Formula Approach, Treasury Plus Formula Approach.

## Marshaling

A rule designed to prevent a secured creditor holding liens on two separate assets from liquidating the one asset that is subject to a second creditor's lien, thereby unfairly leaving that second creditor with no collateral (or less collateral).

The courts have historically given the concept of marshaling limited application, using it only when there are two or more secured creditors of the same debtor (the "common debtor" requirement), when the assets at issue are owned by that common debtor and when no prejudice will accrue to the senior creditor by making it resort to one asset before the other. But some courts (beginning with the oft-criticized *Jack Green* decision in 1979) have expanded the use of marshaling to benefit unsecured creditors' committees and other estate representatives, essentially treating another entity or its property as a second asset and ignoring the "common debtor" requirement of the marshaling doctrine. This usually has been done at the expense of guarantors.

## Mediate Transferee

A transferee who is third or after in a series of transfers, as opposed to an "initial transferee" (who is the first transferee) and an "immediate transferee" of the initial transferee (second in line). The classification is relevant because immediate and mediate transferees may, unlike an initial transferee, escape liability for the transfer if they took for value, in good faith, and without knowledge of the voidability of the transfer.

Bankruptcy Code § 550. See also Immediate Transferee, Initial Transferee, Subsequent Transferee.

**Mediation**

A form of alternative dispute resolution in which a neutral party, the mediator, seeks to promote and assist in negotiating settlement of a dispute. Mediation does not provide a mechanism to compel the parties to settle; any settlement will be the result of a voluntary agreement between the parties. Bankruptcy courts sometimes encourage (to the point of arm-twisting) parties to use mediation.

See also Arbitration.

**Mezzanine Debt**

Loosely applied to a variety of debt other than senior secured debt. Traditionally mezzanine debt is unsecured debt subordinated by its terms to the payment of senior debt. Other types of debt or quasi-debt sometimes described as "mezzanine" include second lien lending and "preferred equity" investments. In the real estate arena a mezzanine debt has come to mean debt secured by ownership interests in the primary borrower (the owner of the property and borrower under the senior loan) rather than the real estate itself.

Mezzanine lenders are often forced in an inter-creditor agreement with the senior lender to waive numerous bankruptcy rights and can end up with fewer rights than other unsecured creditors.

See also A-B Note Structure, Intercreditor Agreement, Second Lien Lending, Subordination, Subordination Agreement.

## Modification of Plan

Before the Chapter 11 plan is confirmed, a pro-ponent of a plan has the right to modify it if the modified plan meets the classification requirements of Section 1122 and the contents of plan requirements of Section 1123. The old plan, as modified, becomes the new plan.

No court approval is needed for the filing of such a modification. But after filing a pre-confirmation modification, the proponent may need to file and distribute to creditors a court-approved disclo-sure statement containing adequate information regarding the modified plan. If the modifications are not material, the court may determine that no further disclosure is necessary. If creditors have voted on the plan prior to modification, the court will usually set a time for creditors to change their votes based upon the plan modification. If creditors do not change their votes, the court will determine acceptance or rejection of the plan based upon their original votes.

After the Chapter 11 plan is confirmed, the pro-ponent of a plan or the reorganized debtor may modify it only if (1) there has not been "substantial consummation," (2) the classification requirements of Section 1122 and the contents of plan requirements of Section 1123 are met, and (3) the court after notice and hearing finds that circum-stances warrant the modification and confirms it under Section 1129 standards. After filing of a post-confirmation modification, the proponent may need to file and distribute to creditors a court-approved disclosure statement containing adequate information regarding the modified plan. If the modifications are not material, the court may determine that no further disclosure is necessary. If creditors have voted on the plan prior to modification, the court will usually set a time for creditors to change their votes based upon the plan modification. If creditors do not change their votes, the court will determine acceptance or rejection of the plan based upon their original votes.

Bankruptcy Code §§ 1101(2), 1127. See also Confirmation, Disclosure Statement, Substantial Consummation.

## Mootness Doctrine

A rule of law, prevalent in appeals, dictating that litigation stop when events have occurred that would render the outcome of the litigation irrelevant. Designed to prevent the needless use of judicial resources. Also referred to as "equitable mootness," but, in the view of aggrieved appellants, a more apt term would be "inequitable mootness."

## Motion for Relief from Stay

A motion requesting the court to terminate, annul, modify, or condition the automatic stay to permit the creditor to take action against a debtor or a debtor's property.

The basic grounds for granting such relief are—(1) for cause, including the lack or adequate protection of an interest in property or (2) against property if the debtor has no equity in the property and the property is not necessary to an effective reorganization.

The lender has additional protection if its collateral is single asset real estate (see Single Asset Real Estate). The court will grant stay relief on single asset real estate collateral not later than 90 days after the order for relief (or such later date as the court determines during this 90 day period) or 30 days after the court determines that the debtor is subject to single asset real estate provisions, unless the debtor has either:

(a) filed a plan of reorganization that has a reasonable possibility of being confirmed within a reasonable time, or

(b) commenced monthly payments equal to interest at the then applicable nondefault contract rate of interest on the value of the creditor's interest in the real estate.

Bankruptcy Code § 362(d). See also Automatic Stay, Necessary To An Effective Reorganization, Single Asset Real Estate.

## Necessary to an Effective Reorganization

A concept in stay relief litigation where a secured creditor seeks relief on the basis that a debtor has no equity in certain property and that the property is not necessary to an effective reorganization. If the creditor can show that the debtor has no equity in the property, the burden then falls to the debtor to show that the property is "necessary to an effective reorganization." This means that the debtor must show not just that the debtor cannot reorganize without the asset in question but also that a reorganization "is reasonably in prospect," meaning, in turn, that there is a decent chance that a plan can be confirmed in the case. In most cases, debtors are given leeway with respect to this burden early in the case, leeway that diminishes with the passage of time.

Bankruptcy Code § 362(d)(2)(B). See also Motion for Relief from Stay.

## New Value

See New Value Defense, New Value Exception, New Value Plan.

## New Value Defense

A defense in preference actions that allows the transferee to avoid liability if it can show that the transferee gave some new consideration to the debtor after the transferee's receipt of the transfer (but only to the extent of the new value given). If the transferee obtained a lien at the time it provided new value, then the defense is not available to the transferee. Also, if the transferee received another avoidable transfer as a result of its giving new value, then the defense is not available to the transferee.

Bankruptcy Code § 547(c)(4). See also Preference.

## New Value Exception

An exception to the absolute priority rule that enables holders of equity to retain their equity interests in the debtor even though a senior non-accepting class has not been paid in full, if the equity holders contribute new capital or other form of acceptable "value" to the debtor.

The rationale for the new value exception (or new value corollary, as it has sometimes been called) is that if the equity holders contribute "new value" under a plan, they are not running afoul of the absolute priority rule's fundamental prohibition of the retention or receipt of property "on account of" their already existing ownership interests in the debtor.

The elements of the new value exception were judicially created and include that the value must, in fact, be "new" (not something that has already been provided by the equity holders), must be in the form of money or money's worth (not in the form of "sweat equity" or some other intangible form of contribution), must be substantial, and must have a value equivalent to or greater than what the equity holder would receive under the plan.

Creditors have routinely attacked new value plans as violating the absolute priority rule, arguing that no matter what new value equity holders propose to contribute, the exclusive opportunity to receive or retain equity interests in the debtor is, in and of itself, property received by the equity holders on account of their existing interests in the debtor. This argument appears to have been accepted by the United States Supreme Court in the *LaSalle* case, at least as to any *exclusive* opportunity provided by a debtor to its equity holders in a plan proposed during the exclusivity period.

Bankruptcy Code § 1129(b)(2)(B)(ii). See also Absolute Priority Rule, Cramdown, *LaSalle* Auction Plan, *LaSalle*, New Value Plan.

**New Value Plan**

A plan of reorganization proposing that original equity holders maintain all or some of their original equity interests, notwithstanding non-acceptance of the plan by a class of unsecured creditors, by contributing "new value" to the debtor.

Bankruptcy Code § 1129(b)(2)(B)(ii). See also Absolute Priority Rule, Cramdown, *LaSalle*, *LaSalle* Auction Plan, New Value Exception.

**Non-Consolidation Opinion Letter**

Another life form bubbling up from the rating agency Petri dish to make a borrower more "bankruptcy remote." A legal opinion that a borrowing entity is a separate, distinct legal entity not subject to consolidation with any affiliate of the borrowing entity. Routinely sought by secured lenders at the outset of securitized lending transactions to obtain assurance that the assets of their borrowers will not be included within the bankruptcy estate of any other entity (or, to have someone to blame, and seek recovery from, if they do).

Non-consolidation opinion letters are not "clean" opinions but "reasoned" opinions running to many pages of discussions and caveats. Despite their limited nature, the rating agencies value them highly and so they have furnished one of the basic foundations upon which a massive securitized lending edifice has been erected in the U.S. Since the consolidation determination is so fact-driven and involves so much discretion from courts possibly operating with a result-oriented motive and at the behest of the major constituencies in the case, few believe that these opinions have much predictive value.

See also Securitization, Special (or Single) Purpose Bankruptcy Remote Entity, Substantive Consolidation.

## No-Shop Clause

A clause in an agreement between a buyer and seller under which the seller agrees not to entertain bids from any other potential buyer. Because no-shop clauses conflict with the debtor/seller's duty to maximize the bankruptcy estate's value and obtain the highest price for its assets, they are disfavored in bankruptcy proceedings.

See also 363 Auction, 363 Sale.

## Non-Impairment Plan

This is an interesting theoretical possibility but is seldom, if ever, actually seen. A plan that does not impair any class of creditors and thus does not have to be accepted by any class of creditors. Such a plan need not comply with the One-Impaired-Class-Must-Accept-The-Plan Rule since there is no impaired class.

While non-impairment generally requires that contractual rights not be altered in any respect, Section 1124 provides that a class of claims can be deemed unimpaired and therefore to have accepted the debtor's plan if the plan:

(1) cures any default (except certain types of defaults need not be cured as noted below);

(2) reinstates the maturity of the claim as it existed prior to the default;

(3) compensates the holder of the claim for any damages incurred in reliance on its right of acceleration; and

(4) compensates the holder of the claim for any actual pecuniary loss incurred in connection with a default of a non-monetary obligation (unless the holder of the claim is an insider or the default arises from failure to operate a nonresidential real property lease); and

(5) does not otherwise alter the legal rights of the holder of the claim.

Certain types of defaults need not be cured in order for the class of claims to be deemed unimpaired—a default that is a breach relating to (1) the insolvency or financial condition of the debtor, (2) the filing of bankruptcy, (3) the appointment of a custodian or the appointment of a trustee in bankruptcy, or (4) satisfying a penalty rate or provision arising from the failure to perform nonmonetary obligations under an executory contract or unexpired lease.

Bankruptcy Code § 1124. See also Acceleration (Reversal Of), Impairment, One-Impaired-Class-Must-Accept-The-Plan Rule.

## Nonrecourse

A secured debt for which the debtor has no liability beyond the value of the collateral pledged. Nonrecourse debt converts to recourse debt in a Chapter 11 case unless the property secured by the debt is sold under Section 363, the property is sold under a plan, or the holder of the debt makes the 1111(b) election.

Bankruptcy Code § 1111(b)(1). See also 1111(b) Election, Exploding Guaranty, Nonrecourse Carveout, Springing Guaranty.

## Nonrecourse Carveout

Loan document provisions that create exceptions to nonrecourse liability. One category of "carveout" is the "bad boy" type of provision, more of an indemnification obligation than an actual recourse liability, where the borrower (and guarantors or indemnitors as well) agrees to cover losses incurred by the lender if, for example, rents or insurance proceeds are diverted or misappropriated. These provisions are to be contrasted with those imposing full "springing" recourse liability if a certain event occurs—typical examples are the filing of a voluntary bankruptcy or violation of transfer restrictions in the loan documents (see Springing Guaranty).

See also Exploding Guaranty, Nonrecourse, Springing Guaranty.

**Nursing Home Revenues**

Income from the operation of a nursing home. Like hotel revenues, these are more properly characterized as accounts than rents. If the lender has failed to perfect under the Uniform Commercial Code by the proper filing of a financing statement, the lender's secured claim is likely to fall victim to the strong arm powers.

Bankruptcy Code § 552. See also Cash Collateral, Hotel Revenues, Strong Arm Powers.

**Offset**

See Setoff.

**One-Impaired-Class-Must-Accept-The-Plan Rule**

The Code requires that if any class is impaired under a Chapter 11 plan, the plan cannot be confirmed unless at least one impaired class accepts the plan (determined without including any acceptances of the plan by insiders). This can be the most difficult of the plan confirmation requirements for a debtor to satisfy, especially in a single asset case, because unlike other obstacles to confirmation such as rejection of the plan by a creditor class, "cramdown" is not available as an end run around this requirement.

Bankruptcy Code § 1129(a)(10). See also Artificial Impairment, Confirmation Requirements, Gerrymandering, Non-Impairment Plan.

## Order for Relief

An order for relief invokes the automatic stay and brings down an iron curtain, separating the pre-bankruptcy from the post-bankruptcy debtor, creating a bankruptcy estate and prohibiting unauthorized transfers of the debtor's property.

The filing of a voluntary bankruptcy petition automatically produces an order for relief. In an involuntary case an order for relief needs to be actually entered by the bankruptcy court. An order for relief will be entered if the debtor does not contest the involuntary petition or, if the debtor contests the involuntary petition, an order for relief will be entered if (1) the court determines that the debtor is not paying its undisputed debts as they come due, or (2) a custodian (other than a trustee, receiver, or agent appointed or authorized to take charge of less than substantially all of the property of the debtor for the purpose of enforcing a lien against such property) was appointed or took possession within 120 days before the petition was filed.

Bankruptcy Code §§ 301(b), 303(h). See also Automatic Stay, Bankruptcy Petition, Involuntary Case, Postpetition Transfer.

**Ordinary Course Defense**

A defense to a preference action under which the defendant must show that the allegedly preferential payment or other transfer to the defendant was made in the ordinary course of business or financial affairs of the debtor and the defendant or made according to ordinary business terms.

Bankruptcy Code § 547(c)(2). See also Preference, Preference Action.

**Ordinary Course Professionals**

Attorneys, accountants and other professionals employed by the debtor to perform non-bankruptcy related services necessary or appropriate to the debtor's ordinary business operations. Although it is generally thought that such professionals do not constitute the type of "professional persons" whose employment and compensation must be approved by the bankruptcy court, debtors nevertheless routinely file motions seeking the court's permission to employ them.

See also Professional Persons.

**Oversecured Creditor**

A secured creditor whose collateral is worth more than its claim. To the extent that the lender is oversecured, the lender is entitled to an allowed secured claim not just for the amount it is owed as of the commencement of the case but also for interest on its claim and for any reasonable fees, costs, or charges provided for under its loan documents. But oversecured status can be an impediment in stay relief litigation because the creditor cannot show that the debtor has no equity in the property.

Bankruptcy Code §§ 361, 362(d)(2), 506. See also 506(b), Adequate Protection, Stay Relief, Undersecured Creditor.

## PACA

PACA-MAN devours all comers!

Acronym for Perishable Agricultural Commodities Act. Federal legislation that provides suppliers of certain agricultural products with extraordinary protections that sometimes bedevil a debtor's other creditors, even its secured lenders. If a supplier meets the PACA requirements, the products it delivers (and the proceeds of those products including inventory, accounts receivable, and cash derived from the products) are treated as though they are the supplier's property rather than the debtor's property, the debtor holds them in trust for the benefit of the supplier, and the supplier's claim trumps the lender's otherwise superior lien on the products.

## Perfected

The act of establishing the priority of the secured creditor's lien or security interest above other interests in collateral for a debt. If not properly perfected, the lender's lien or security interest will encounter The Terminator—the Strong Arm

Powers—that allow the estate to avoid unperfected liens and to retain avoided liens for the benefit of the estate.

See also Avoidance Actions, Strong Arm Powers, Unperfected.

## Perishable Agricultural Commodities Act

See PACA.

## Personal Service Contract

Term often used to describe a contract that cannot be assigned because one of the parties is uniquely positioned, to the exclusion of all others, to perform it.

For example, a contract with Picasso to produce a work of art cannot be assigned to someone else to perform even if the contract does not expressly prohibit assignment. Section 365 recognizes this concept, and even broadens it considerably, by prohibiting "the trustee" (which usually also includes the debtor in a Chapter 11 case) from assuming or assigning a contract where "applicable law excuses a party, other than the debtor, to such contract or lease from accepting performance or rendering performance to an entity other than the debtor or the debtor in possession, whether or not such contract or lease prohibits or restricts assignment of rights or delegation of duties..." This language not only covers the Picasso situation but many others where state or federal law prohibits assignment. Ironically, it has also been interpreted by some courts to prevent the debtor, in this example Picasso himself, from assuming the contract in his bankruptcy case.

Bankruptcy Code § 365(c). See also Assumption and Assignment of Executory Contracts and Unexpired Leases.

## Petition

See Bankruptcy Petition.

## Plan

See Chapter 11 Plan.

## Postpetition

- The period of time starting with the filing of the debtor's bankruptcy petition.

See Involuntary Bankruptcy Petition, Order for Relief, Voluntary Bankruptcy Petition.

## Postpetition Financing

See DIP Financing.

## Postpetition Interest

What every secured lender wants but what it gets only when it is oversecured.

Although oversecured lenders are often able to negotiate payment of postpetition interest, most courts hold that only accrual is required until the interest exhausts the lender's equity "cushion" and eliminates the oversecured status because the lender's "cushion" itself is not entitled to adequate protection.

Bankruptcy Code § 506(b). See also Adequate Protection, Equity Cushion, Oversecured Creditor, Single Asset Real Estate, Undersecured Creditor.

## Postpetition Transfer

Transfer of property of the estate occurring after entry of the order for relief in the bankruptcy case. Avoidable and subject to recapture by the debtor, trustee, or other estate representative if not authorized by the Code or court order.

Bankruptcy Code § 549. See also Avoidance Action.

## Preference

A payment or other transfer by a debtor to or for the benefit of a creditor for an already existing debt made while the debtor was insolvent (or that rendered the debtor insolvent) and that enabled the creditor to receive more than it would have received in a liquidation of the debtor's assets.

Generally, transfers made within 90 days prior to bankruptcy may qualify as preferences. But if the transfer is made to or for the benefit of an insider of the debtor, the transfer may qualify as a preference if it was made within one year prior to the bankruptcy.

A transferee often escapes liability in a preference action by successfully asserting one or more of the defenses provided by the Code (see, e.g., New Value Defense and Ordinary Course Defense).

Fully secured creditors or oversecured creditors cannot be liable for preferences because the trustee will not be able to establish that the creditor received more by virtue of the transfer than the lender would receive in a liquidation.

A preference suit is maddening from a creditor's perspective because the creditor is often still owed money by the debtor and yet is being sued for receiving some portion of what the creditor was rightfully owed in the first place.

Bankruptcy Code § 547. See also Avoidance Action, Insider, New Value Defense, Ordinary Course Defense, Oversecured, Preference Action, Undersecured.

## Preference Action

A lawsuit brought by the debtor, trustee, or other representative of the bankruptcy estate to avoid and recover a preference.

See also Avoidance Action, Preference.

## Preferential Transfer

See Preference.

## Prenegotiated Plan

A Chapter 11 plan that has been negotiated with the major constituency or most of the major con-stituencies prior to filing. Unlike a Prepackaged Plan, the Prenegotiated Plan is not immediately ready toconfirm and must pass through the disclosure statement process and usually some additional voting process and negotiations or perhaps even a contested confirmation.

See also Prepackaged Plan.

## Prepackaged Plan

A bankruptcy plan approved by the debtor's creditors before the debtor files its bankruptcy petition. Sometimes referred to as a "prepack." The "prepack" can allow a debtor to begin and end the formal bankruptcy process in just a few days. It is usually employed when a debtor can obtain a majority in number and two-thirds in amount of acceptances from each class but not the unanimous acceptance that would be required to alter contractual rights outside of bankruptcy.

Prepackaged plans are favored by creditors and other parties in interest as a means of streamlining the bankruptcy process and reducing the expense of Chapter 11.

See also Acceptance of Plan, Accepting Class, Confirmation Requirements, Cramdown, Prenegotiated Plan.

## Prepayment Consideration

The proper way (along with the terms "Yield Maintenance" and "Call Protection") for the lender to describe the lender's contract-based right to receive additional compensation if the debtor pays the loan before the maturity date.

"Prepayment consideration" is to be contrasted with a phrase that should never be uttered by a lender—"prepayment penalty."

Courts are split on whether and under what circumstances prepayment consideration is allowed as part of the lender's claim. Prepayment consideration is typically calculated by determining the interest that would have been payable to the lender over the remaining life of the loan, deducting the amount the lender can realize by investing the prepaid amount at the then-prevailing treasury rate over the same term, and making a further present value deduction to take into account the lender's receipt of its principal at the time of prepayment rather than at the time of maturity. This calculation is designed to protect the benefit of the bargain the lender struck when it negotiated for compensation (in the form of interest) in exchange for the use of its money. But prepayment consideration is criticized on various grounds, including that the calculation formula usually assumes that the money will be reinvested at the U.S. Treasury rate even where it is clear that the lender can and will be able to obtain a higher rate of return on reinvestment.

See also Defeasance, Oversecured Creditor, Prepayment Penalty.

**Prepayment Penalty**

The term used by a debtor (and the term that should never be used by a lender) to describe the increased amount due when the debtor repays the lender early. Debtors argue that such "penalties" are unenforceable under state law and under the Code.

See also Prepayment Consideration.

**Prepetition**

The period of time before the filing of the debtor's bankruptcy petition.

**Preservation of Lien for Benefit of the Estate**

The transfer of an "avoided" lien to the estate so that the estate and its general creditors benefit from the value of the lien. This prevents a junior secured creditor from ascending to a more senior position and obtaining an undeserved windfall in the form of the value generated by the lien avoidance.

Bankruptcy Code § 551. See also Avoidance Actions, Strong Arm Powers.

**Presumptive Contract Rate Approach**

One of the methods that bankruptcy courts use to set the cramdown interest rate that a bankruptcy plan must pay to a secured creditor that does not accept the plan. Under this approach, the rate established by the pre-bankruptcy loan documents is presumed to be the appropriate cramdown interest rate. The secured creditor is permitted to rebut the presumptive rate by showing that interest rates or other costs have increased since the making of the contract. The debtor may rebut the presumptive rate by showing that interest rates or costs have decreased.

See also Coerced Loan Approach, Cost of Funds Approach, Cramdown, Cramdown Interest Rate, Forced Loan Approach, Formula Approach, Market Rate Approach, Prime Plus Formula Approach, Treasury Plus Formula Approach.

**Prime Plus Formula Approach**

One of the methods that bankruptcy courts use to set the cramdown interest rate that a plan must provide to an objecting secured creditor. Under the prime plus formula approach, the court starts with prime as a base rate and then adjusts that rate upward by assessing the risk associated with the facts of the case. The risk premium is determined by reference to such factors as the debtor's credit history, the nature of the collateral, the length of repayment, and the viability of the reorganization plan.

See also Coerced Loan Approach, Cost of Funds Approach, Cramdown, Cramdown Interest Rate, Forced Loan Approach, Formula Approach, Market Rate Approach, Presumptive Contract Rate Approach, Treasury Plus Formula Approach.

**Priming Lien**

A lien securing a postpetition credit extension that is senior or equal to a lien already attached to some or all of the debtor's property. The bankruptcy court may not authorize a priming lien unless it finds that the debtor is unable to obtain credit otherwise and that the existing lienholder's interest in its collateral is adequately protected notwithstanding the grant of the priming lien.

Like the Loch Ness Monster, the true priming lien is much feared but seldom actually sighted and is doubted by some to exist at all.

Bankruptcy Code § 364(d)(1). See also Adequate Protection, DIP Financing.

## Priority Claim

An unsecured claim that is entitled to be paid after secured creditors but before other unsecured creditors—for example, administrative claims, wage claims, and tax claims.

Bankruptcy Code § 507. See also Administrative Claim, Superpriority Claim.

## Priority Unsecured Claim

See Priority Claim.

## Proceeds

Items that "proceed from" other items. Inventory produces proceeds in the form of accounts, an account produces proceeds in the form of cash, etc.

While Section 552 terminates after-acquired property provisions of security agreements, it affirms the continuing application of the lender's prepetition security interest to the "proceeds" of its collateral.

Bankruptcy Code §§ 363(a), 552. See also After-Acquired Property Clause, Equities of the Case.

## Professionals' Fees

Compensation paid to professional persons employed in a Chapter 11 case. Such compensation is subject to bankruptcy court approval, and professionals' fees are allowable only for actual, necessary services and only to the extent that the fees are reasonable.

Bankruptcy Code § 330(a). See also Professional Persons.

## Professional Persons

Persons employed by the debtor, trustee, or a committee to represent or serve the debtor in some capacity in its bankruptcy case on bankruptcy-related matters, including attorneys, accountants, appraisers, and auctioneers, and sometimes brokers, investment bankers, and other consultants. Their engagement and compensation is subject to bankruptcy court approval and scrutiny.

Bankruptcy Code § 327(a). See also Administrative Claims, Attorneys' Fees, Ordinary Course Professionals, Professionals' Fees.

## Proof of Claim

A document filed with the bankruptcy court by a creditor that substantiates its claim against the debtor. It asserts the amount, nature, and priority of the claim.

See also Allowed Claim.

## Property of the Estate

All of the debtor's property as of the bankruptcy filing, including tangible and intangible property, and all legal and equitable interests in property. Very intentionally broadly defined in order to bring the greatest possible amount of the debtor's property into the bankruptcy estate.

Bankruptcy Code § 541. See also Custodian, Motion for Relief from Automatic Stay, Turnover.

## Proponent

The party proposing a Chapter 11 plan. The debtor is usually the sole plan proponent in a case, but secured lenders and committees also sometimes file plans.

See also Chapter 11 Plan, Competing Plan.

## Reasonably Equivalent Value

One of the elements that the plaintiff must prove in a fraudulent transfer lawsuit. Determined by a bankruptcy judge who some suspect has a bias in favor of the bankruptcy estate and against the fraudulent transfer defendant, a judge who possesses perfect 20-20 hindsight and a second-guessing ability of truly heroic proportions.

Bankruptcy Code § 548(a). See also Avoidance Action, *BFP*, Constructively Fraudulent Transfer, *Durrett,* Insolvent, Value.

## Receiver

A supposedly disinterested person appointed by a state or federal non-bankruptcy court to administer a borrower's property prior to the filing of a bankruptcy case. Although the Code prohibits the appointment of a receiver in a bankruptcy case, Section 543 permits the court to allow a receiver appointed prepetition to remain in place during the bankruptcy case if the court finds that the interests of creditors are better served by permitting the receiver to remain in place. Because creditors have been increasingly successful in keeping receivers in place postpetition, creditors and debtors now frequently engage in a race to two courthouses—the creditor racing to a non-bankruptcy court to seek appointment of the receiver—and the debtor racing to bankruptcy court to obtain the benefits of the automatic stay before a receiver can be appointed.

Bankruptcy Code §§ 105(b), 543. See also Custodian.

## Recharacterization

The treatment by a court of a transaction or document according to its "true" substance rather than the form used by the parties.

A court may order that a loan to an entity be treated as an equity contribution if the "loan" bears the characteristics of an equity contribution rather than a true loan (as where the loan was made by an insider, there is no maturity date, there are no scheduled payments on the loan, and/or the borrower is undercapitalized).

A transaction characterized by the parties as a sale may be recharacterized as a secured transaction if, for example, the seller retains possession of the property sold, with the buyer being entitled to the property only if the seller defaults on a debt to the "buyer."

An "absolute" assignment of rents will often be treated as creating merely a lien in favor of the lender assignee.

A leases are also subject to recharacterization if the lease terms resemble the terms of a secured trans-action rather than a true lease.

See also Absolute Assignment of Rents, Assignment of Rents for Security, Disguised Financing, Equitable Subordination, True Lease, True Sale.

## Reclamation

A seller's right to recover possession of goods sold to an insolvent buyer under the Uniform Commercial Code or common law. The right of reclamation survives, in modified form, in the debtor/purchaser's bankruptcy filing.

Under most state laws the demand for reclamation must be in writing and made within 10 to 20 days of the debtor's receipt of the goods. The seller's state-law right of reclamation continues in bankruptcy, as modified under Section 546(c), and the seller may reclaim goods received by the debtor while the debtor was insolvent, if received by the debtor within 45 days before the date of the bankruptcy filing. The seller, however, must demand reclamation in writing no later than 45 days after the debtor received the goods (or no later than 20 days after the bankruptcy filing if the 45-day period expires after the filing of the bankruptcy case).

The right of reclamation is subordinate to a prior security interest in the goods sought to be reclaimed. Sellers of goods whose reclamation rights are denied may still be able to assert an administrative claim under Section 503(b)(9) for goods delivered within 20 days of the filing of the bankruptcy case.

Bankruptcy Code §§ 503(b)(9), 546(c). See also Administrative Claim.

133

## Recoupment

A defense to a claim allowing the defendant to reduce the amount it must pay to the plaintiff by the amount that the plaintiff owes to the defendant in connection with the contract or transaction on which the plaintiff seeks recovery.

The right of recoupment is similar to the right of setoff but with three important distinctions. First, recoupment is available to a creditor seeking to offset prepetition debts against postpetition debts. By contrast, setoff is not available to a creditor under such circumstances because it applies only to an attempted setoff of prepetition debts against prepetition debts (or postpetition debts against post-petition debts). Second, recoupment is available to the creditor only if the mutual obligations arise from the same contract or transaction, a limitation not applicable to a creditor's right of setoff. Third, a creditor may exercise recoupment without seeking the bankruptcy court's permission, while the creditor cannot exercise its right of setoff without first obtaining relief from the automatic stay.

Bankruptcy Code § 553 . See also Automatic Stay, Setoff.

## Recourse

The right of a creditor to recover the debt it is owed from a debtor's assets other than the specific collateral pledged to secure the debt. An otherwise non-recourse claim is converted to a recourse claim in Chapter 11.

Bankruptcy Code § 1111(b). See also Nonrecourse.

## Regularly Conducted Foreclosure Sale

A foreclosure sale of real estate held in accordance with applicable state law and without an element of improper collusion that could have the effect of "chilling" the purchase price at the sale. The U.S. Supreme Court's *BFP* decision held that such a sale cannot be a fraudulent transfer no matter how low the purchaser bids at the sale. The court in the *BFP* case stated that its holding extended only to real estate foreclosure sales.

See also *BFP* Case, Constructively Fraudulent Transfer, *Durrett* Case, Reasonably Equivalent Value.

## Rejection Claim

The claim of the non-debtor party to a contract or lease that is rejected by the debtor. Rejection of an executory contract or unexpired lease is treated as a prepetition breach of the contract or lease by the debtor, entitling the non-debtor party to a damages claim for the breach. The amount of some rejection claims is subject to a statutory cap under Section 502(b).

Bankruptcy Code § 503(b)(6). See also Landlord Claim, Rejection of Executory Contracts and Unexpired Leases.

## Rejection of Plan

A vote against a Chapter 11 plan.

Bankruptcy Code § 1126(a). See also Acceptance of Plan, Confirmation Requirements.

## Rejection of Executory Contracts and Unexpired Leases

A right provided to the debtor under Section 365 to rid itself on a prospective basis of executory contracts and unexpired leases that the debtor believes are not beneficial to the bankruptcy estate. Rejection of an executory contract or unexpired lease is treated as a prepetition breach of the contract or lease by the debtor, entitling the non-debtor party to a damages claim for the breach.

Bankruptcy Code § 365(a). See also Assumption and Assignment of Executory Contracts and Unexpired Leases, Landlord Claim.

## Relief From Stay

See Motion for Relief from Stay.

## REMIC

Acronym for Real Estate Mortgage Investment Conduit, a creature of the Internal Revenue Code that allows the holder of securitized mortgages, usually a trust, to avoid entity-level or "double" tax on the income from the mortgages owned by the REMIC.

A REMIC is subject to numerous restrictions that could complicate Chapter 11 cases and even cause Chapter 11 filings. For example, a REMIC cannot allow a significant modification of a mortgage except under narrowly defined conditions, so the debtor's only means of obtaining such a modification may be to impose the modification under a Chapter 11 plan. As for complications, for example, a REMIC cannot hold more than a *de minimis* amount of assets other than real estate or real estate mortgages, creating potential difficulties if a Chapter 11 plan proposed to distribute equity interests in the debtor in satisfaction of some or all of the mortgage debt.

## Reorganization

The effort of a debtor under Chapter 11 to restructure its debts, remain in possession of its property, confirm a plan, and pay its debts on the terms stated under a confirmed plan.

## Reorganization Plan

See Chapter 11 Plan, Liquidating Plan.

## Reorganized Debtor

The debtor under a confirmed Chapter 11 plan.

See also Debtor, Debtor in Possession.

## Replacement Lien

A postpetition lien provided to a lender covering property acquired by the debtor after the bankruptcy filing.

Lenders are often entitled to adequate protection of their interests in collateral, especially where the debtor proposes to use or sell the collateral. Section 361 describes various means for providing adequate protection, including replacement liens. A replacement lien is especially important to a lender whose loan is secured in whole or in part by inventory and accounts that are consumed in the debtor's Chapter 11 operations. Since Section 552 cuts off the lender's security interest in inventory and accounts generated postpetition, the lender soon would have no collateral left. Instead, the lender is given a "replacement lien" in inventory and accounts generated after the Chapter 11 filing to "replace" what the lender has lost by the debtor's consumption of its prepetition collateral. Unfortunately for the lender, the "replacement" may not be a dollar-for-dollar equivalent of what has been consumed.

Bankruptcy Code §§ 361(2), 552(a). See also Adequate Protection, Indubitable Equivalent, Reverse Alchemy.

### Retirees' Committee

A committee appointed to represent the interests of the debtor's non-union retirees.

Bankruptcy Code § 1114(d). See also Committee.

### Reverse Alchemy

The conversion of gold into base metal.

See, for example, Adequate Protection, Eat Dirt Plan, Indubitable Equivalent, Replacement Lien.

## Ride Through

An executory contract that is neither rejected (including a deemed rejection) nor assumed in the bankruptcy case is said to "ride through" the case and continue to be binding on both the debtor and non-debtor party as if the bankruptcy case had not been filed.

See also Assumption and Assignment of Executory Contracts and Unexpired Leases, Rejection of Executory Contracts and Unexpired Leases.

## Roll-Over

Application of a lender's postpetition loan to pay prepetition debt owed to the lender, effectively cross-collateralizing the lender's prepetition and postpetion debt. The prepetition debt is said to be "rolled over" to become postpetition debt.

See also Cash Collateral, Cash Collateral Order, DIP Financing, Replacement Lien.

## Room Revenues

See Hotel Revenues, Nursing Home Revenues.

## Rule of Explicitness

A judicial doctrine that prevents a junior creditor under a subordination agreement from being forced to give up its distributions under a bankruptcy plan to pay interest to the senior (but undersecured) creditor under the agreement unless the subordination agreement specifically requires that result.

An unsecured (or undersecured) creditor is not entitled to payment of interest on its claim in bankruptcy. But senior creditors argued that they could be paid postpetition interest on their claims—not from the *debtor*, but out of bankruptcy plan distributions that otherwise would have been paid to the junior creditors under the subordination agreements. This argument rested on language commonly included in subordination agreements providing that the junior creditor is not entitled to any payment until the senior creditor is paid in full. The courts found it unlikely that junior creditors would, under this language, anticipate being forced to hand over their bankruptcy plan distributions to a senior creditor to pay postpetition interest on the senior creditor's unsecured claim, and therefore developed the rule that the junior creditor under a subordination agreement will not be required to give up its bankruptcy plan distributions to pay postpetition interest to the senior creditor unless the subordination agreement clearly provides that result by, for example, explicitly stating that if the borrower files bankruptcy, the senior lender is entitled to payment of interest from bankruptcy plan distributions that would otherwise be paid to the junior creditor.

Bankruptcy Code § 510(a). See also A-B Note Structure, Second Lien Lending, Subordination Agreement.

**Rules**

See Federal Rules of Bankruptcy Procedure.

## Sale Free and Clear

A sale under Section 363 that takes advantage of the provisions of Section 363(f) allowing the property to be sold "free and clear of any interest in such property" under specified conditions including, most importantly, in the case of a lien, when "the price at which such property is to be sold is greater than the aggregate value of all liens on such property." Any liens then attach to the proceeds of the sale.

There is controversy over whether the Code requires that the sale price be for the entire amount of the liens even if the property is of less "value" than the aggregate amount of the liens.

*Diabolical Question: Is "amount" a synonym for "value" in any Thesaurus published in the Upper World? Isn't the undersecured lender fully protected by its right to credit bid the entire amount of its debt?*

Some bankruptcy courts have stretched the notion of "interests in such property" to include unsecured claims, such as tort claims and other claims that might be asserted against the buyer on the theory of successor liability, and have purported to bar the future assertion of such claims against both the property sold and the buyer.

Bankruptcy Code § 363(f). See also 363 Auction, 363 Sale, Credit Bid Rights, Sale Order, Successor Liability.

## Sale-Leaseback

A sale of property where the owner simultaneously leases it back from the buyer. Such a transaction can be vulnerable to recharacterization as a loan rather than a lease. If, considering the transaction as a whole, the seller/lessee is deemed to have transferred all significant risks and rewards of property ownership to the buyer/lessor, the transaction will be entitled to treatment as a lease under the Code. That treatment is more favorable because the debtor cannot modify the terms of a true lease under a Chapter 11 plan, while the terms of a debt obligation (including a lease recharacterized as a debt) can be modified under a plan. Further, the debtor is obligated to stay current on postpetition non-residential real estate lease obligations during the pendency of its bankruptcy case. By contrast, lenders often receive no payment at all until after confirmation of a plan.

Bankruptcy Code § 365(d)(3). See also Disguised Financing, Recharacterization, True Lease, True Sale.

**Sale Order**

The order entered by the bankruptcy court approving and authorizing a 363 sale. The order is usually drafted by the buyer and often includes provisions making the sale free and clear not just of liens and interests but of various "claims" such as successor liability claims and perhaps even recoupment rights and other defenses of parties to contracts assigned as part of the sale.

See also 363 Auction, 363 Sale, Sale Free and Clear.

**Schedules**

Documents that the debtor must prepare, in an officially prescribed format, and file with the bankruptcy court listing the debtor's assets, contracts, leases, debts and other information relating to the debtor. The term "schedules" is often used inclusively to refer also to the debtor's Statement of Financial Affairs, another document that the debtor must prepare and file in an officially prescribed format.

See also Statement of Financial Affairs.

## Second Lien Lending

While there have always been junior secured creditors, in the first decade of the 21st century an entire specialized line of lending business on a second lien basis has developed and become more and more formalized and differentiated from traditional mezzanine lending. The basic differences between second lien lending and mezzanine lending are that second lien lending is secured (though "mezzanine" debt is itself often secured in some fashion), usually uses LIBOR as a reference rate, and has traditionally been cheaper than mezzanine debt (though increases in LIBOR beginning in 2005 have closed the gap between the two). Also, the second lien lender usually enjoys a more favorable intercreditor agreement with the senior lender than the mezzanine lender (for example, the second lien lender does not usually have to agree not to receive payments if the senior loan is in default) but still must waive certain of its rights in bankruptcy.

While a second lien lender's collateral will often include real estate, this form of financing has not migrated in this variation to the real estate lending arena. But see A-B Note Structure.

See also Intercreditor Agreement, Mezzanine Debt, Subordination.

## Secured Claim

A claim against the debtor secured by collateral or by a right of setoff against the debtor. A secured creditor retains its prepetition lien or right of setoff notwithstanding the bankruptcy filing, and the debtor must provide adequate protection to the lender as a condition of using the lender's collateral during the bankruptcy case. A Chapter 11 plan must provide for payment in full of all secured claims, with interest, as a condition of confirmation, and a secured creditor is entitled to credit bid if there is a sale of its collateral either during the case or under the plan.

Bankruptcy Code § 506(a). See also 363 Auction, 363 Sale, Adequate Protection, Allowed Claim, Avoidance Action, Credit Bid Right, Oversecured Creditor, Preference, Recoupment, Setoff, Strong Arm Powers, Surcharge, Undersecured Creditor, Valuation of Collateral.

## Secured Creditor

A creditor that holds a secured claim.

## Secured Tax Claim

Once upon a time secured tax claims furnished a wonderful way to satisfy the One-Impaired-Class-Must-Accept-The-Plan Rule (by stretching out their payment or paying them less interest than they might otherwise be entitled).

But this tactical maneuver is no longer available because the BAPCA amendments require that a Chapter 11 plan provide for payment of a secured tax claim under the same rules that govern unsecured priority tax claims. Accordingly, a secured tax claim cannot be impaired and must be paid no later than five years after the bankruptcy filing and on terms no less favorable than the most favored nonpriority unsecured claim provided for by the plan (with the exception of the treatment to the administrative convenience class under Section 1122(b)).

Bankruptcy Code § 1129(a)(9)(C), (D). See also BAPCA, Confirmation Requirements, One-Impaired-Class-Must-Accept-The-Plan Rule.

## Securitization

Refers broadly to the practice of transforming financial assets, such as accounts, notes, and mortgages, into securities, either as a debt offering or as a "true sale." The investment banks and credit rating agencies "tranch" the securities from AAA downward with each descending class being subordinate in certain respects to the class above it. Real estate-related securities are referred to as CMBS or Commercial Mortgage Backed Securities. Care is taken to make the securitization vehicle and the entities that transfer loans into it "bankruptcy remote."

The basic securitization document is a Pooling & Servicing Agreement (often referred to as the "PSA") establishing a trust for the benefit of the investors. The loans are administered by a Trustee, a Master Servicer, and a Special Servicer. The Special Servicer will be the one representing the securitization trust when the loan becomes troubled in some way. Some think this arrangement will create complications similar to those that cropped up in the old RTC days, but the real complexity will probably derive instead from the Byzantine loan structures being created with layers of senior debt, subordinate debt, preferred equity, etc.

A newcomer in this area is the CRE (Commercial Real Estate) CDO (Collateralized Debt Obligation).

See also Collateralized Debt Obligations, Commercial Mortgage Backed Securities, Intercreditor Agreement, Mezzanine Debt, REMIC, Special (or Single) Purpose Bankruptcy Remote Entity.

## Serial Filing

A debtor's filing of one or more successive bankruptcy petitions after the filing of its initial bankruptcy petition.

See also Chapter 20, Chapter 22.

## Setoff

The right of a creditor to reduce a debt it owes to the debtor by the amount the debtor owes to the creditor. The Code upholds a creditor's right to offset mutual prepetition debts (a creditor is not permitted to offset a prepetition debt against a postpetition debt), and provides the creditor with a secured claim to the extent of its setoff right. The creditor's right of setoff spares it from paying its debt to the debtor in "real" dollars while receiving in return an unsecured claim paid, if at all, from the debased currency of distributions under the debtor's Chapter 11 plan (which are likely to be less than 100 cents on the dollar). A creditor must usually obtain relief from the automatic stay before exercising setoff (but see Financial Markets Contracts).

Bankruptcy Code §§ 506(a), 553. See also Motion for Relief from Stay, Oversecured Creditor, Recoupment, Secured, Secured Claim, Secured Creditor, Undersecured Creditor.

## Settlement Agreement

A contract between two or more parties to resolve a pending dispute. Upon filing its bankruptcy petition, a debtor is no longer authorized to enter into a binding settlement agreement without approval of the court.

## Shopping Center

See Shopping Center Lease.

## Shopping Center Lease

A lease at a shopping center that is afforded special and relatively favorable treatment under the Code (see Shopping Center Lease Provisions). The Code itself does not define the term. Courts have used the following factors to determine if a lease is a "shopping center lease": whether there is a combination of leases of various types of tenants at the center; whether all leases are held by a single landlord; whether the various tenants at the center are engaged in the commercial retail distribution of goods; whether there is a common parking area at the center; whether the premises were purposefully developed as a shopping center; whether there is a master lease; whether there are fixed hours during which all stores are open; the existence of joint advertising; contractual interdependence of the tenants as evidenced by restrictive use provisions; the existence of percentage rent provisions in the leases; the right of tenants to terminate their leases if the anchor tenant terminates its lease; joint participation by tenants in trash removal and other maintenance; the existence of a tenant mix; and whether stores at the center are contiguous.

See also Adequate Assurance, Assumption and Assignment of Executory Contracts and Unexpired Leases, Shopping Center Lease Provisions.

## Shopping Center Lease Provisions

Code provisions creating special protections for shopping center landlords. A debtor, whether as landlord or tenant, is permitted to assume and assign leases (see Assumption and Assignment of Executory Contracts and Unexpired Leases). A requirement for assumption and assignment is that the debtor must show that the non-debtor party to the lease will have "adequate assurance" of the future performance of the lease by the assignee.

Although the Code does not define the term "adequate assurance" with respect to leases generally, it does define the term with respect to a shopping center lease. The lessor must receive adequate assurance: (1) of the source of rent and other consideration due under the lease, and in the case of an assignment, that the financial condition and operating performance of the proposed assignee and its guarantors, if any, is similar to the financial condition and operating performance of the debtor and its guarantors, if any, as of the time the debtor became the lessee under the lease; (2) that any percentage rent due under the lease will not decline substantially; (3) that assumption or assignment of the lease is subject to all the provisions of the lease, including (but not limited to) provisions such as a radius, location, use, or exclusivity provision, and will not breach any such provision contained in any other lease, financing agreement, or master agreement relating to the shopping center; and (4) that assumption or assignment of the lease will not disrupt any tenant mix or balance in the shopping center.

Bankruptcy Code § 365(d)(3). See also Assumption and Assignment of Executory Contracts and Unexpired Leases, Shopping Center, Shopping Center Lease.

**Single Asset Real Estate**

Real property that is a single property or project (other than residential real property with fewer than four residential units). To qualify as single asset real estate, the property must generate substantially all of the gross income of a debtor and there must be no substantial business conducted there other than the business of operating the real property and conducting activities incidental to the operation of the real property.

A lender with a lien on single asset real estate receives special protections under the Code and may obtain relief from the automatic stay if the debtor fails to, within 90 days after commencement of the case, file a plan of reorganization that has a reasonable possibility of being confirmed within a reasonable time or fails to start making interest payments to the lender.

If there is a dispute as to whether the real estate qualifies as single asset real estate, then the debtor must file a plan or start making payments of interest to the lender as stated above within 30 days after the bankruptcy court determines that the property is single asset real estate. Under new provisions introduced by BAPCA, the burden is on the lender to bring the issue of "single asset real estate" status before the court if the debtor denies in its schedules that its property is single asset real estate.

Courts have held that hotels, nursing homes, marinas, and similar operations that involve an active business other than operation of the real estate itself do *not* constitute single asset real estate.

Bankruptcy Code §§ 101(51D), 363(d)(3).

**Single Purpose Entity**

See Special (or Single) Purpose Bankruptcy Remote Entity.

**Small Business Case**

A Chapter 11 case in which the debtor is a small business debtor.

Bankruptcy Code § 101(51D). See Small Business Debtor.

## Small Business Debtor

A debtor engaged in commercial or business activities whose aggregate, non-contingent liquidated secured and unsecured debts as of the date of the bankruptcy filing are $2,000,000 or less. The $2,000,000 cap excludes debts owed to affiliates or insiders of the debtor.

Chapter 11 contains special provisions designed to facilitate reorganizations in smaller cases by streamlining the process ordinarily applicable to a Chapter 11 debtor. For example, in the Chapter 11 case of a small business debtor the process for confirmation of a bankruptcy plan is more flexible, the bankruptcy court may order that no disclosure statement is necessary, the hearing on approval of the disclosure statement and plan may be combined, and the timing for a hearing to approve the plan is put on a faster track than in an ordinary Chapter 11 case. These benefits come at a price, however, as a small business debtor is subject to additional reporting and oversight provisions not applicable in other Chapter 11 cases.

If a creditors' committee is appointed in the debtor's case, the debtor will no longer be considered a small business debtor unless the court determines that the creditors' committee is not sufficiently active and representative to provide effective oversight of the debtor.

A debtor whose primary activity is the business of owning or operating real property or activities incidental to owning or operating real property will not qualify as a small business debtor even if the debtor would otherwise meet the definition of a small business debtor.

Bankruptcy Code § 101(51D). See also Small Business Case.

## SNDA

Acronym for Subordination, Nondisturbance, and Attornment Agreement.

See Subordination, Nondisturbance and Attornment Agreement.

## Solicitation

The act of requesting an acceptance or rejection of a Chapter 11 plan. Solicitation of acceptances or rejections of a plan are permitted only after distribution of a court-approved disclosure statement.

See also Acceptance, Adequate Information, Disclosure Statement, Rejection.

## Special (or Single) Purpose Bankruptcy Remote Entity

A borrower whose bankruptcy is supposedly "remote" because (1) its purpose is limited by its organizational documents, usually to the operation of a single real estate asset, (2) it agrees not to incur debt other than first mortgage debt, deeply subordinated secondary debt, and a limited amount of trade debt, and (3) it agrees to a number of "separateness" covenants to minimize the chance that the borrower's assets and liabilities will be intermingled with the assets and liabilities of any entity affiliated with the borrower.

These measures help limit the number of potential creditors that might force the borrower into an involuntary bankruptcy and minimizes the possibility that the borrower will be substantively consolidated with an affiliate of the borrower in the affiliate's bankruptcy. In some cases the vote of an "independent director" is required for the borrower to file

154

a bankruptcy case.

The possible bankruptcy of the borrower is made even more remote (and many believe this will be the most important of all of these devices in preventing a Chapter 11 filing) by requiring the debtor's principals to sign a guaranty providing for "springing recourse" (full personal liability) if a bankruptcy occurs.

See also Exploding Guaranty, Nonrecourse, Recourse, Springing Guaranty, Springing Recourse, Substantive Consolidation.

## Springing Guaranty

A guaranty where the guarantor's liability is triggered by a bankruptcy filing by the borrower, a failure to obtain dismissal by the borrower of an involuntary bankruptcy petition filed against it, or other conditions specified in the guaranty. Probably far more effective to prevent a bankruptcy filing than the independent director, nonconsolidation opinion, and other trappings of bankruptcy "remoteness" developed by the credit rating agencies.

See also Exploding Guaranty, Special (or Single) Purpose Bankruptcy Remote Entity.

## Springing Recourse

Nonrecourse debt instruments sometimes include a provision purporting to convert the instrument to recourse upon the filing of a bankruptcy case against the debtor. This is probably an unenforceable *ipso facto* clause under Section 365(e)(1). Note that this is unlike a Springing Guaranty where the debtor's filing creates recourse for a third party guarantor and not the debtor itself. Note also that such a "springing recourse" provision is sometimes unnecessary in Chapter 11 because, under certain circumstances, Section 1111(b)(1)(A) converts nonrecourse debt to recourse for purposes of a Chapter 11 case. But Section 1111 does not confer that benefit in a Chapter 7 case where the springing recourse provision would be invalidated by Section 365(e)(1), preventing the creditor from sharing in any distribution of property of the estate other than its own collateral.

See also Exploding Guaranty, *Ipso Facto* Clause/Provision, Special (or Single) Purpose Bankruptcy Remote Entity, Springing Guaranty.

**Stalking Horse**

The use of the term in the bankruptcy context does not carry the connotation of "decoy" or "deceit" that it carries outside of bankruptcy. It refers instead to the initial proposed purchaser in a 363 auction process whose deal with the debtor is subject to higher and better offers. The stalking horse usually negotiates a break-up fee and other bid protections to compensate itself in case it is not the successful purchaser of the debtor's assets.

See also 363 Auction, 363 Sale, Bid Protections, Break-Up Fee.

**Stamp Tax**

For those who thought that the American Revolution was fought to escape this type of tax, it still exists and is collected in many states by the sale of stamps that are required to be attached to certain transaction documents such as deeds or mortgages before the documents may be recorded.

Transfers under a confirmed Chapter 11 plan may not be taxed under any law imposing a stamp tax or "similar" tax under Section 1146(a) (see Transfer Tax). But purchasers in Section 363 bankruptcy sales have attempted to expand Section 1146(a), with some controversy, to sales occurring before a Chapter 11 plan is filed or confirmed, arguing that such a sale is in contemplation of a Chapter 11 plan.

Bankruptcy Code § 1146(a). See also Transfer Tax.

## Statement of Financial Affairs

A document to be completed and filed by the debtor on a designated official form listing information about the debtor such as: the debtor's gross income for the two years before the bankruptcy filing; transfers by the debtor to creditors in the 90 days before the bankruptcy filing and transfers to creditors who are insiders of the debtor within one year before the bankruptcy filing; identification of all bookkeepers and accountants for the debtor for the six year period before the bankruptcy filing; a statement of the dollar amount of the debtor's last two inventories taken before the bankruptcy filing; and a listing of the debtor's partners, officers, directors and significant stockholders.

Bankruptcy Code § 521(a)(1). See also Schedules.

## Statutory Lien

A lien arising solely by force of a statute or a "lien of distress for rent" (whether or not statutory). The term does not encompass consensual liens (including UCC security interests) or judicial liens. Statutory liens are often afforded to warehousemen, innkeepers, public or common carriers, agisters (livestock grazers if you didn't know), garagemen, vehicle repairmen, hospitals, attorneys, landlords, and taxing authorities. Statutory liens are avoidable by the debtor under a variety of circumstances under Section 545.

Bankruptcy Code §§ 101(53), 545.

## Stay

See Automatic Stay.

## Stay Relief

Get Out Of Jail (But Not For Free) Card.

An order of the bankruptcy court granting a creditor or other party "relief" from the constraints of the automatic stay. It is not free because it is obtained, if at all, usually only after one or more contested hearings where the creditor must prove such things as its lack of adequate protection, that the debtor has no equity in the collateral, or that other "cause" exists to justify the relief. Diabolically, once lifted, the stay may be reimposed, and if the debtor confirms a plan before the creditor has foreclosed, the plan will control disposition of the property. Once stay relief is obtained, the moving party is free to enforce its state law rights and remedies or to otherwise act, free of the stay, to the extent authorized by the bankruptcy court.

Bankruptcy Code § 362(d). See also Automatic Stay, Motion for Relief from Stay.

## Stay Relief Motion

See Motion for Relief from Stay.

## Strong Arm Powers

The right of a debtor to avoid unperfected liens and other transfers through the Code-created mechanism of allowing the debtor to assume the status of a hypothetical lien creditor or bona fide purchaser of real estate. The strong arm powers are also frequently employed to avoid unperfected security interests and unrecorded real estate liens. The strong arm powers allow the debtor to avoid transfers by using state fraudulent transfer statutes that usually have longer look-back periods than the two year Code provision.

Bankruptcy Code § 544. See also Bona Fide Purchaser, Fraudulent Transfer, Hypothetical Lien Creditor, Perfected.

## *Sub Rosa* Plan

Latin term meaning something of a more unpleasant fragrance concealed "under the rose." This is a Bogeyman of the bankruptcy world—rumored to exist but few confirmed sightings since the *Lionel* case in 1983. This doctrine, applied, the authors believe, by only two bankruptcy courts in published case history, holds that a 363 sale that, in practical effect, resolves the entire bankruptcy case constitutes a *sub rosa* plan of reorganization—that is, an impermissible attempt to evade the requirements and difficulties of the plan confirmation process.

The doctrine is no longer living in anything but name, but still haunts the dark corners of our psyches. The worry is needless, however, as bankruptcy practitioners quickly discovered how to slay this Bogeyman—by distributing proceeds from the sale only pursuant to a "liquidating" plan of reorganization proposed and confirmed after the sale.

See also Liquidating Plan.

## Subordination

One creditor's lien or claim being rendered inferior to another, usually by voluntary agreement but sometimes by judicial decree.

Bankruptcy Code § 510. See also Equitable Subordination, Intercreditor Agreement, Subordination Agreement.

## Subordination Agreement

An agreement between two creditors in which one creditor subordinates (or confirms the existing subordination of) its lien or the payment of its claim, or both, to the lien or payment in full of the claim, or both, of the other creditor. The subordination features *per se* of such an agreement are enforceable in a bankruptcy case under Section 510, while other provisions of the subordination agreement may or may not be enforceable.

Bankruptcy Code § 510(a). See also Intercreditor Agreement, Rule of Explicitness, Subordination.

## Subordination, Nondisturbance and Attornment Agreement

An agreement between a borrower's tenant and the borrower's lender in which the parties agree, among other things and with varying degrees of complexity, that the tenant will attorn (become a tenant of a new landlord) to the lender and that the lender will not disturb the rights of the tenant under the lease if through foreclosure or deed-in-lieu the lender succeeds to ownership of the property. Feared by many lawyers to be an executory contract that can be rejected in the tenant's or landlord's bankruptcy.

See also Executory Contract, Leasehold Mortgage, Rejection of Executory Contracts and Unexpired Leases.

## Subrogation Rights

The right of an insurer, guarantor or other surety, after paying a claim of a creditor for which the debtor was primarily liable, to "step into the shoes" of that creditor, including any security for the debt, and to collect from the debtor the amount paid. Subrogation rights are upheld, with some modification, under Section 509(a). But as provided at Section 507(d), a subrogee does not inherit the priority status of certain claims otherwise entitled to priority (such as priority wage claims under Section 507(a)(3), priority employee benefits claims under Section 507(a)(4), and priority tax claims under Section 507(a)(8)).

Bankruptcy Code §§ 502(e)(1)(C), 507(d), 509(a). See also Co-Debtor, Guarantor.

## Subsequent Transferee

An immediate transferee or any mediate transferee.

See also Immediate Transferee, Initial Transferee, Mediate Transferee.

## Substantial Consummation

One devoutly to be wished by some but not by others. Section 1101(2) defines substantial consummation as "(a) transfer of all or substantially all of the property proposed by the plan to be transferred, (b) assumption by the debtor or by the successor to the debtor under the plan of the business or of the management of all or substantially all of the property dealt with by the plan, and (c) commencement of distribution under the plan." Courts have generally interpreted this provision very expansively. Upon substantial consummation, those objecting to the plan and attempting to prosecute appeals to overturn the plan's confirmation are likely to fall victim to the mootness doctrine. The plan proponents usually very devoutly wish for the moment of substantial consummation, and for this favor they must pay the very small price of being unable to modify the plan thereafter.

Bankruptcy Code §§ 1101(2), 1127(b). See also Equitable Mootness, Modification of Plan, Mootness Doctrine.

## Substantive Consolidation

The thing that thousands of legal opinions have assured "would" not be done but might be done anyway—the combination of the assets and liabilities of two separate legal entities, usually affiliated ones (parent-sub, sub-parent, brother-sister entities, including non-debtor entities), treating them as a single debtor.

See also Administrative Consolidation.

## Successor Liability

Liability imposed on the purchaser of assets for claims against the prior owner of the assets. The courts originally developed this doctrine to protect victims of personal injury torts, especially future tort claimants, where there has been a "*de facto* merger" or "mere continuation" of the old business by the new owner of the assets. There has been some recent extension, though less so than is generally thought, of this doctrine to include debts to providers of goods, services, or capital (lenders) to the old business.

Purchasers in section 363 sales usually attempt to include provisions in sale orders purporting to protect themselves against successor liability. Such provisions are usually unopposed, primarily because the potential victims of such provisions, many of whom have not even been injured yet, are not present in court to defend their rights. Some courts refuse to approve such provisions "on their own motion." Even where they are initially approved by the bankruptcy court, other courts sometimes refuse to enforce them later, notwithstanding the mootness doctrine, often citing the theory that the bankruptcy court did not have jurisdiction to deprive parties of their claims without giving them an opportunity to be heard (see Due Process).

Bankruptcy Code § 363. See also 363 Auction, 363 Sale, Sale Free and Clear, Sale Order.

## Superpriority Claim

A priority claim with priority over all other priority claims. A superpriority claim under Section 507(b) can be trumped only by a Section 364(c)(1) priority claim (a priority claim granted to a lender to induce it to make an unsecured postpetition loan to the debtor—this creature, like a priming lien, is virtually nonexistent). All superpriority claims, including "super" superpriority claims under Section 364(c)(1), are unsecured and do not prime secured claims.

Lenders almost always insist that cash collateral and DIP financing orders specify that the lender will have a superpriority claim to the extent that the "adequate protection" granted to the lender under such an order proves to be inadequate. But Section 507(b) automatically provides a superpriority claim where adequate protection fails, even if the lender's cash collateral order or DIP financing order does not mention the lender's entitlement to such a claim.

Bankruptcy Code §§ 364(c)(1), 507(b). See also Adequate Protection, Administrative Expense Claim, Cash Collateral Order, DIP Financing Order, Priming Lien, Priority Claim.

### Superpriority Lien

See Priming Lien.

### Surcharge

An assessment payable from a creditor's collateral of the reasonable, necessary costs incurred by the bankruptcy estate to preserve or dispose of the collateral. The assessment is limited to the extent of the benefit realized by the creditor. Creditors sometimes consent to a surcharge of their collateral, but the court has the power to surcharge the creditor's collateral over its objection.

Bankruptcy Code § 506(c). See also Carveout, Cash Collateral Order, DIP Financing Order.

## Surety

A person or entity, including a guarantor, that agrees to be responsible for the debt of another. A surety has subrogation rights, entitling the surety to step into the shoes of the creditor to the extent it pays the debtor of the primary obligor, and those rights are recognized, with limitations, in bankruptcy.

See also Co-Debtor, Subrogation Rights.

## Thermidorean Reaction

The overthrow and execution of leftist Maximillien Robespierre and his allies by rightist deputies in the French National Convention on 9 Thermidor (French revolutionary calendar), 1794. Often used to describe a period of conservative reaction following a period of liberal or radical leftist ascendancy.

See also BAPCA.

## *Till* Case

See Cramdown Interest Rate.

## Topping Fee

In a 363 auction a type of break-up fee that the debtor agrees to pay to an initial proposed purchaser (the stalking horse) if the proposed purchaser is not the prevailing bidder in the auction. A topping fee is calculated as a percentage of the difference between the stalking horse's initial offer and the final bid price paid for the assets.

See also 363 Auction, 363 Sale, Bid Protections, Break-Up Fee, Stalking Horse.

## Trade Creditor

Holder of a general unsecured claim arising from the provision of goods or services to the debtor (in contrast especially to an undersecured lender holding an unsecured deficiency claim).

Under BAPCA, trade creditors now hold administrative expense claims for the value of goods they deliver to a debtor in the ordinary course of the debtor's business within 20 days before the commencement of the bankruptcy case.

Bankruptcy Code § 503(b)(9). See also Administrative Expense Claim, BAPCA, General Unsecured Claim, Reclamation Claim.

## Transfer

A transfer of the debtor's property or an interest in the debtor's property to another party. The Code defines "transfer" as the creation of a lien or security interest, the retention of title as a security interest, the foreclosure of a debtor's equity of redemption, or any other mode, direct or indirect, absolute or conditional, voluntary or involuntary, of disposing with property or an interest in property.

To illustrate how broad the concept can be, the revocation of a SubChapter S Election has been deemed to be a transfer (of possible tax benefits or attributes from the corporate debtor to its shareholders).

Transfers by the debtor are subject to rigorous scrutiny in bankruptcy, and the broad definition of "transfer" helps to ensure that all transactions affecting the debtor's property or its interests in property can be examined to determine whether they are subject to avoidance as preferences, fraudulent transfers, or otherwise.

Bankruptcy Code § 101(54). See also Fraudulent Transfer, Postpetition Transfer, Preferential Transfer.

## Transfer Tax

Taxes sometimes imposed on purchasers or other recipients of interests in real property when evidence of those interests is recorded in the office of the recorder of deeds. Recording taxes have been interpreted to be a form of "stamp tax or similar tax" under Section 1146(a). But purchasers in 363 sales have attempted to expand Section 1146(a), with some controversy, to sales occurring before a Chapter 11 plan is filed or confirmed, arguing that such a sale is in contemplation of a Chapter 11 plan.

Bankruptcy Code § 1146(a). See also Stamp Tax.

## Transferee

The recipient of a transfer. Section 550 differentiates between initial, immediate and mediate transferees for purposes of avoidance actions, and generally provides greater protections to subsequent transferees than it does to a party who is the first ("initial") transferee from the debtor.

Bankruptcy Code § 550. See also Fraudulent Transfer, Initial Transferee, Mediate Transferee, Preference, Subsequent Transferee.

## Treasury Plus Formula Approach

One of the methods that bankruptcy courts use to set the cramdown interest rate that a plan must provide to an objecting secured creditor. Under the treasury plus formula approach, the court starts with the treasury rate as a base rate and then adjusts that rate upward by assessing the risk associated with the facts of the case. The risk premium is determined by reference to such factors as the debtor's credit history, the nature of the collateral, the length of repayment, and the viability of the reorganization plan.

See also Coerced Loan Approach, Cost of Funds Approach, Cramdown, Cramdown Interest Rate, Forced Loan Approach, Formula Approach, Market Rate Approach, Presumptive Contract Rate Approach, Prime Plus Formula Approach.

## True Lease

A lease that has the characteristics of an operating lease, as opposed to a lease that has the characteristics of a financing.

Courts look to a number of factors to distinguish "true leases" from leases that are disguised financing transactions. The determination usually hinges on whether the term of the lease is materially less than the useful life of the leased property and whether the lessee must pay the fair market value of the property to acquire it during or at the end of the lease term.

If the agreement is found to be a true lease, then the debtor's right to modify the terms of the transaction are limited. The debtor may assume or reject the lease but may not (absent the lessor's consent) modify the terms of the lease. If the lease is found to be a disguised financing, and the lessor-creditor has properly perfected its lien or security interest, the bankruptcy court will treat the "lease" as creating a lien or security interest in favor of the "lessor" and treat the "lessor" as a secured party or mortgagee, with the debtor being treated as owner of the "leased" property. If the lien or security interest was not properly perfected, it may be avoided by the debtor under the strong arm powers, leaving the "lessor"/secured creditor with an unsecured claim.

See also Disguised Financing, Recharacterization, Sale-Leaseback, True Sale.

## True Sale

A sale of property that is determined by a bankruptcy court, using 20-20 hindsight, to have characteristics evidencing the intent of the buyer and seller to enter into a "true" sale of the property, transferring all of the seller's interest in the property to the buyer. A "true" sale is often described as having transferred all of the significant risks and rewards of ownership to the buyer. In contrast, a transaction may be called a "sale" by the parties but recharacterized by the court as something else where, for example, the "sale" does not sufficiently transfer the risks and rewards of ownership to the buyer. Such a transaction creates, at best, a lien in favor of the "buyer."

In the seller/debtor's subsequent bankruptcy proceeding, property that the debtor sold in a true sale is no longer property of the bankruptcy estate and is not protected by the automatic stay. But if the sale is not "true," the property remains property of the debtor's bankruptcy estate and is subject to the automatic stay. The "buyer" is treated as a creditor with a claim that will be subject to treatment in a plan. Also, if the lien was not properly perfected, the debtor may use its strong arm powers under Section 544 to avoid the lien.

See also Recharacterization, Sale-Leaseback, Securitization.

**Trustee**

See Chapter 7 Trustee, Chapter 11 Trustee, and United States Trustee.

In Chapter 11 cases where the debtor remains in possession and control of its property, the debtor (with minor exceptions) has the rights, powers, and functions of a trustee appointed under the Code. The Code often references only the rights and functions of "the trustee," but in Chapter 11 cases those references should be read to say "the trustee or debtor in possession."

Bankruptcy Code § 1107. See also Debtor in Possession.

**Turnover (of Property of the Estate)**

The transfer of property of the estate by a person in possession of the property to the debtor or trustee. Under Section 542 parties in possession of property of the bankruptcy estate are required to deliver that property to the debtor or the trustee. Used by some devilish debtors and trustees to sue for recovery of accounts receivable.

Bankruptcy Code §§ 542, 543. See also Receiver.

**Undersecured Creditor**

A creditor whose collateral is worth less than its claim. If a lender is undersecured, its claim, for bankruptcy purposes, is divided into a "secured claim" equal to the value of its collateral and an "unsecured claim" for the deficiency. But see 1111(b) Election.

Bankruptcy Code § 506(a). See also Oversecured Creditor, Secured Claim, Unsecured Claim, Valuation of Collateral.

**Unexpired Lease**

A lease to which the debtor is a party and whose term has not expired. A debtor may assume, or assume and assign, only those leases that are unexpired. The bankruptcy filing does not extend the term of a lease.

The Code pointlessly adds the adjective "unexpired" when referring to lease but not to executory contracts.

Bankruptcy Code § 365. See also Assumption and Assignment of Executory Contracts and Unexpired Leases, Rejection of Executory Contracts and Unexpired Leases.

## Unfair Discrimination

Singling out one or more creditors for less favorable treatment than other creditors holding similar claims. Debtors sometimes attempt to give such treatment to the lender's unsecured deficiency claim by, for example, paying the claim on terms less favorable than provided for unsecured creditors generally. Section 1129(b)(1) precludes confirmation of plans that unfairly discriminate (unless all classes accept their treatment under the plan, including any unfair discrimination).

Bankruptcy Code § 1129(b)(1). See also Confirmation Requirements, Gerrymandering.

## Unimpaired

See Impaired Class, Impairment.

## United States Trustee

An employee of the U.S. Department of Justice charged with responsibility for oversight of various matters pertaining to bankruptcy cases generally, including the appointment of members to committees.

The presence of the U.S. Trustee in business bankruptcies is often felt most acutely on issues such as conflicts of interest pertaining to the eligibility of law firms and other professionals to serve as advisers to the debtor or a committee. The U.S. Trustee is also often to be found objecting to various aspects of fee applications filed by professionals for the debtor and committees.

The hall monitor of the bankruptcy process.

## Unliquidated Claim

A claim whose dollar amount has not been determined and is not easily determinable. Courts are in disagreement as to whether a debt is unliquidated when a dispute regarding liability or amount exists.

## Unperfected

The status of a lien or other interest on real property that has not been properly recorded. Also the status of a security interest in personal property where the creditor has not filed a financing statement or otherwise taken steps required under state law to make the security interest effective against third parties.

See also Perfected, Strong Arm Powers.

## Unsecured Claim

A creditor who does not hold a lien, mortgage, or other security for its claim.

See also Secured Claim, Trade Creditor, Undersecured Creditor, Valuation of Collateral.

## Unsecured Creditors' Committee

See Committee, Creditors' Committee.

## Use of Cash Collateral

Concept vital to the debtor, as its cash is its lifeblood as it attempts to reorganize under Chapter 11. To use its cash in bankruptcy, the debtor must obtain either court approval or the consent of its secured lender if the cash is subject to the lender's lien. Where the secured lender does not consent, the case's first battle is often fought at a cash collateral hearing conducted just after the bankruptcy filing in which the creditor tries to prove that its interest in the cash is not adequately protected or that the cash does not belong to the debtor at all.

Bankruptcy Code § 363. See also Absolute Assignment of Rents, Adequate Protection, Assignment of Rents for Security, Cash Collateral.

## U.S. Trustee

See United States Trustee.

## Valuation of Collateral

The bankruptcy court's determination of the value of the lender's collateral controls, among other things, the amount of the lender's secured claim (and, if undersecured, its unsecured claim) and whether the lender will be entitled to interest and attorneys' fees while the bankruptcy case is pending.

Bankruptcy courts value a lender's collateral for various purposes and at different times in the case. The court-determined value will often depend on whether the court uses liquidation value or going concern value for the lender's collateral.

At the outset of a case the court may value the lender's collateral to determine whether the lender is adequately protected from potential losses resulting from the debtor's proposed use of the lender's collateral during the course of the case. If the court finds that the lender has a large "equity cushion" (the value of the collateral in excess of the lender's debt), the court may determine that the equity cushion, by itself, adequately protects the lender's position.

Collateral valuation also controls whether the lender will be entitled to postpetition, pre-confirmation interest on its claim because only oversecured creditors are entitled to such interest.

Finally, a Chapter 11 plan must provide for payment in full, with interest, of a secured creditor's secured claim, and the valuation process will determine the amount of that claim.

Bankruptcy Code § 506(a), (b). See also Adequate Protection, Deficiency Claim, Equity Cushion, Going Concern Value, Liquidation Value, Market Value, Oversecured Creditor, Secured Claim, Undersecured Creditor, Unsecured Claim.

## Value

The consideration that a transferee of property from the debtor provides to the debtor in exchange for the transfer. Where the debtor does not receive *reasonably equivalent* value in exchange for a transfer, the transfer is subject to avoidance as a fraudulent transfer (see Constructively Fraudulent Transfer).

In the context of a fraudulent transfer action under Section 548, the concept of "value" means, in addition to the obvious concept of *property* that the creditor provides to the debtor, the "satisfaction or securing of a present or antecedent debt of the debtor." Accordingly, a lender gives "value" in exchange for the debtor's payment of a debt to the lender if the lender applies that payment to satisfy the debtor's debt. Where the debtor transfers to the lender an interest in the debtor's property in the form of a lien on the debtor's property, the lender is said to have given "value" in exchange for that transfer by securing the debtor's debt with the lien (which makes perfect sense, since the debtor could have instead liquidated the property rather than providing a lien against it and then used the proceeds to make a payment against the debt).

Even in the case of a payment made by the debtor to satisfy antecedent debt, the transfer to the lender could theoretically be a constructively fraudulent transfer if the "value" supplied by the lender was not "reasonably equivalent value." For example, if the lender accepted a $100 payment from the debtor but reduced the debtor's debt by less than $100, a bankruptcy court might find that the debtor received less than reasonably equivalent value.

Bankruptcy Code § 548(d)(2)(A). See also Constructively Fraudulent Transfer, Fraudulent Transfer, Intentionally Fraudulent Transfer, Reasonably Equivalent Value.

## Voluntary Bankruptcy Petition

A bankruptcy petition filed by the debtor, as contrasted with an involuntary bankruptcy petition filed against the debtor by its creditors.

Bankruptcy Code § 301. See also Bankruptcy Petition, Involuntary Bankruptcy Petition, Involuntary Case.

## Withdrawal of Reference

Transfer of bankruptcy litigation or the bankruptcy case itself from the bankruptcy court to the United States district court.

Withdrawal of reference, although it rarely occurs, can be a valuable procedural device for a lender or other party that finds itself as a defendant in a bankruptcy-related case and that prefers to litigate the dispute in the United States district court rather than in what may be perceived as a biased bankruptcy court. The district court can take control of a case related to a Chapter 11 case or even an entire Chapter 11 case by withdrawing reference of the case from the bankruptcy court.

Bankruptcy Code 28 U.S.C. § 157(d).

## White Knight

As in non-bankruptcy mergers and acquisitions, a party that infuses capital into or purchases outright a failing debtor, thereby "saving the day" for (or, sometimes, prolonging the agony of) the debtor and its creditors.

See also 363 Auction, 363 Sale.

## Yield Maintenance Provisions

See Prepayment Consideration.

## Zone of Insolvency

A kind of "twilight zone" somewhere near actual insolvency or maybe even all the way there. In any event a very dangerous place for officers and directors of the debtor, and increasingly their professionals, where their fiduciary duty extends to creditors as well as to the owners of the debtor.

See also Insolvent, Deepening Insolvency.